Slurls

They Called Their Website WHAT?!

The World's Worth Internet URLs
from effoff.com to penisland.net

Andy Geldman

ANGEL INTERNET PRESS
LONDON, ENGLAND

Published by Angel Internet Press
an imprint of Angel Internet Ltd
Angel Internet Ltd
PO Box 57672
London
NW7 0EP
www.angel-internet.com/aip

ISBN: 978-0-9565330-0-5

Cover photograph © iStockphoto.com/ImageegamI

From the moment I picked your book up until I laid it down, I was convulsed with laughter. Someday I intend reading it.

Groucho Marx

Contents

Welcome to Slurls

Would you book a holiday through *oldmanshaven.com*? Or visit *ipwine.com* for a bottle of Chardonnay? Would you download music from *mp3shits.com*? These are Slurls: outrageous website addresses (URLs) innocently chosen by real businesses.

Organisations of every type have chosen URLs with unintentional double meanings. The sports team of Marist College (in New York) are known as the Red Foxes, so *GoRedFoxes.com* makes perfect sense—but most visitors see *Gored Foxes* staring back at them. A directory of Californian counsellors registered *therapistfinder.com* and called themselves *Therapist Finder*; others only saw *The Rapist Finder*. If you want to find a celebrity's agent, naturally you ask "who represents . . . ?" But set up your agent-finder business at *whorepresents.com* and people will think you sell *Whore Presents*.

How did this happen? Well, the founders of the internet needed an address system, and they came up with domain names: the telephone numbers of the net, used in website addresses and after the "at" symbol in email addresses. Bafflingly, they ignored a thousand years of Western convention and decided we didn't need spaces in domain names.* In fact, the only characters that are allowed are letters, numbers, full stops, and hyphens.

---

* Also, spaces are used in computer programming to separate commands, so URLs with spaces would send geeks into impotent tantrums. We can't have that.

In a world without spaces, we mentally insert our own. And you might not stick yours where I stick mine. Spaces, that is. If you've spent years working for a worthy kids' charity like *The Children's Laughter Foundation*, when someone shows you *childrenslaughter.com*, you imagine giggling little scamps and feel a warm glow inside. Everyone else sees something entirely different—something that only inhabitants of high-security mental hospitals get a warm fluffy feeling thinking about.

So *Slurls* is about Whore Presents, Gored Foxes, Rapist Finders and other unsavoury combinations. I'm probably quite unique in the world, because I view those unholy unions with great fondness. But please don't freak out; I can explain myself.

I used to commute to work on the London Underground: two hours of daily misery in dirt, noise, heat and—worst of all—hordes of other grumpy travellers. A happy bunch we were not. One thing relieved the tedium: the free Metro newspaper handed out at the station. For me, the bizarre "funny old world" stories were the highlight.

In February 2006 the Metro ran a piece about website addresses with accidental double meanings. It was the funniest thing I'd seen in years and introduced me to the prostitute gifts, pervert detectors and unlucky foxes that I now look back on with such nostalgia. Most people would enjoy the article, tell their friends, then forget all about it. I'm different. You see, I'm a geeky programmer and I knew it was within my power to find more of these hilarious URLs.

That same day I coined the Slurls name by combining slur*
with URL, set up a website, and started blogging under the name
"Chief Slurler". I used this pseudonym so I could show it off to
colleagues without revealing I created the site myself during
work hours. They weren't taken in. Oddly, my boss wasn't
annoyed, just impressed that I had done it so quickly.

I have collected Slurls ever since, in the same way other
(more normal) people collect stamps or Beanie Babies. If I'm
lucky, visitors to the website suggest them. More often, I spend
hours searching forums and blogs. Either way, I find 'em, list 'em
and, ahem, make up puerile jokes about 'em.

Before we continue, I must thank the owners of these
unfortunate URLs for giving so much joy to the world. Please
don't be upset—it's all just a bit of fun. But for heaven's sake,
stick a hyphen in there and you're all fixed. Oh, and welcome to
Slurls!

---

* To garble your words like a drunk—just as the words in URLs are run
together without spaces.

The Nature of the Beast

Slurls are rare animals, found cowering in the dark damp recesses of the web. It's not always easy to tell if the quivering creature in front of you is the real deal, so how do you know for sure? Luckily, you don't have to lift its tail and inspect its orifices—there are a few simple rules to follow:

a. **There's a website**. Seems obvious, but I've known chancers to stick a couple of words together and expect a prize. If I can't see it in my web browser address bar it doesn't count.

b. **It's an active website**. Sometimes sites are under construction, full of ads, or just empty. The website needs to be used for something.

c. **There's a double meaning**. *Buttpaste.com* may raise a smile but it's not a Slurl because it can only be read one way. What the hell is Butt Paste anyway? It's a delicately-named brand of American nappy rash cream. Obviously.

d. **It's not deliberate**. Some cheeky scamps choose a naughty name on purpose, but they usually give the game away by joking about it. An example: Colorado off-license *beaverliquors.com* has licking lips animations and sells t-shirts. Busted.

It's worth mentioning a special breed that ploughs its own furrow (wouldn't you if you could?) The last rule is broken and instead we get:

e. **It's a fake Slurl**: a website created just to convince people that a real business has unwittingly chosen a filthy domain name. Yes, there are people whose lives are so desperately empty they will do that for a giggle. They tend to give it away with in-jokes, and merchandise posing as product samples or corporate souvenirs. More on the fakes later.

Hunting Slurls might seem silly, but to me it's a serious business and I have standards to maintain. I only deal in Slurls of quality: well-groomed, healthy specimens with real words and good spelling. But sometimes in exceptional circumstances I will overlook a little text-speak or other abomination. If you think I've pushed the boundaries too far, by all means get in touch and I will take your feedback very seriously, before concluding that I know better. And if it's decency whose boundaries you think are straining then it's probably best not to bother.

A word of warning: don't worry if you feel a nagging urge to look up the URLs in this book—it's quite normal. But check yourself for a moment before acting on that burning sensation.* Granted, there's nothing more satisfying in life than seeing a

---

* After all, it could be cystitis.

naughty phrase in your browser's address bar, coupled with a deadpan website about widget manufacture. But sometimes, sadly, site owners come to their senses and change their website's address—a selfish act sure to disappoint eager visitors. But there is still hope: if you can't get to an URL listed here in the normal way, take a look at *slurls.com*, where I've done my damnedest to capture screenshots of these wonderful websites in their prime. While they might not have the impact of the real thing, they do evoke the carefree spirit of the times.

That's all you need to know. I'll start the tour nice and slow before we move onto the more exotic cases. Let's get stuck in!

CHAPTER ONE

Never Precede an Exchange
or Express With an "S"

S hopping is a grim pastime. First you use the roads: half are full of tailgating psychopaths, and the other half are solid with congestion. If you beat the odds and get to the shops alive, you have to contend with elbows in the ribs and umbrella spokes in the eyes. To add insult to injury, there's excruciating boredom while you actually *wait* to hand over your hard-earned cash. With the chore done you battle home, weeping, bruised and blinded, then realise you've forgotten the essential purchase you went out to get. But you did manage to buy a load of useless junk.

It's all different on the internet. The second you need something you go to a friendly online retailer (effortlessly guided there by Google), choose and pay in seconds, and have the goods delivered to your door within a couple of days. It's with quiet confidence that so many online shops call themselves "express". There's Cycle Express, Bathroom Express, Party Dress Express and many more. Sadly, the Loch Ness Express has closed down, and neo-Nazis never got the Rudolf Hess Express off the ground. But you get the idea.

Exchanges are also big online. At an exchange you can trade directly with other web users around the world: the democracy and power of the internet at its best. Exchanges are ideal for finding hard-to-find items and stone-cold bargains (common translation: stolen goods). Lots of sites call themselves something-exchange. For example, at Knowledge Exchange the trade is in ideas, Horse Exchange needs no explanation, and Cellar Exchange is for wine collectors. But I'm hard-pressed to get the point of the Child Care Exchange—if I look after your kid and you look after mine, other than being a bit more inclined to lock them in a cupboard, aren't we back where we started?

Anyway, that's what this chapter is about, the two most common breeds of Slurl: exchanges and expresses.

A Trifle Strange

The OddsExchange website shows which online bookmaker has the best betting odds for thousands of different sporting events.

www.oddsexchange.com

The company has a unique way of describing what they do. In their own words:

"[OddsExchange] allows its user to be in touch with the whole world of bets being aware of any change, even of the slightest trifle."

Thank God that's all cleared up. What's that? It doesn't make any sense? I'll explain: the site lists the best betting odds, even if they're better by the smallest weeniest trifle with a miniscule cherry on top. Imagine the smallest trifle you can, then imagine another one a hundred times smaller, and you still won't be near the trifle size they use. Let's move on.

The company behind OddsExchange is based in Malta, an island nation in the Mediterranean Sea. Mysteriously, the server running the web site is in Liechtenstein, a tiny country sandwiched between Switzerland and Austria, like a miniscule wiener in a pair of oversized lederhosen. Liechtenstein is even smaller in size than the trifles that are now the international standard unit for betting odds.

Besides tax evasion and money laundering, Liechtenstein is known for making concrete fastening systems and false teeth. No, really. Probably in the same factory, with a little corner set aside for odd sex changes (is there any other kind?)

I Wish I'd Been a Girlie, Just Like My Dear Papa

The Lumberman's Exchange is a marketplace for lumberjack equipment, traded by both professional dealers and individual tree-bashers.

www.lumbermansexchange.com

It's hard to imagine a more comically appropriate example of how not to name an online exchange. Is it possible that the logging industry insiders behind the site hadn't heard of *The Lumberjack Song*, one of Monty Python's best known sketches? In the original skit a barber confesses to always wanting to be a lumberjack, then is joined in a forest by a troupe of Canadian Mounties for a good old sing-song.

It goes awry when he starts singing about skipping, flowers, and hanging around in bars dressed as a woman. The final revelation, that he wishes he had been a girl, disgusts the Mounties and breaks his sweetheart's heart. It's a scene played out the world over by tragic individuals trapped in the wrong body, well, except for the whole lumberjack, Mounties and singing thing. Did The Lumberman's Exchange not see a teeny-weenie connection? Or they just thought it would be fine and no-one would notice?

The Lumberjack Song has been performed countless times for TV, film and stage—sometimes with special guests, including George Harrison and Tom Hanks. It has been performed in

German by the Pythons themselves, adapted for a Spanish audience, and has enjoyed thousands of impromptu renditions at talent shows, karaoke, and any other time people have felt the urge. Personally, I burst into the song if someone so much as wears a checked shirt and stands under a tree.

The Lumberman's Exchange had a change of heart around 2003 and moved the site to lbxonline.com. *Spoilsports.*

Get Your Motor Running

To my way of thinking, "sex press" is the perfect term for a company that publishes its pornography on old-fashioned tree guts rather than in bits and bytes. Internet filth is a roaring success, but printed porn is languishing, so I was surprised to find a business still plugging away at this URL:

www.exoticcarsexpress.com

I wonder, what kind of rag does the Exotic Car Sex Press publish? To keep up with internet competitors it must be something new and spicy. Obviously it involves cars, but motor vehicles and mating have always gone together* so how can they jazz it up a bit?

Well, they could feature people having sex *in* cars. But that's so last week: the "dogging" craze of sex in car parks and other public places hit the British tabloids in 2003. It's still going strong, but don't confuse longevity with fashion—some people still have mullets.

Maybe they cover people having sex *with* cars? Yawn. Edward Smith from Washington State has had sex with a thousand cars, and his current girlfriend is a white Volkswagen

---

* I don't have any evidence for this, unless you count Kate and Leo's steamy sex scene in *Titanic*. Even so, early cars looked like sofas on wheels (think Chitty Chitty Bang Bang) so I'm sure one was christened pretty early on.

Beetle named Vanilla. He also sees a 1973 Opal GT called Cinnamon, and a 1993 Ford Ranger Splash named Ginger, the big slag. It's true! It was on telly and everything. Well, Channel Five.

OK, here's something really different: *cars having sex with cars.* Yeah, that's what I call exotic! Not only is it completely new, but there's scope for a full range of sub-perversions. How about a dirty old Transit van getting it on with a pair of giggly young Fiestas? Some nasty tailpipe action with a twin-exhaust Golf GTI? Or really push the boundaries: a Porsche 911 getting a thorough servicing from an assembly-line robot: oil change and everything, phooar! Yes, that *must* be it.

So, why does the website feature photos of unviolated sports cars? Why does it waffle on about the Exotic Cars Express? And—let's get down to basics here—why is it the website for a Miami-based transporter of luxury cars? What a waste of a good URL.

There is but one glimmer of hope—a photo of a limited-production $500,000 sports car, captioned "Your Toy, Our Joy". It sounds like they've hired serial car-molester Edward Smith, and he's playing some sneaky spanner-hockey away from his usual garage. Now really Edward, doesn't Vanilla have enough to put up with?

Publish and Be Damned

Childs Express is a delivery company located in Baltimore. They have been providing delivery, moving and storage services for four generations. On their home page they proudly display their first non-horse-drawn vehicle, along with two generations of Childs's in the business. A true family firm, still going strong after all these years. Something to be proud of. Here's something they shouldn't be proud of:

```
www.childsexpress.com
```

When Mr Childs set up his delivery company he didn't know that a century later, in an uninvented and unimaginable medium, spaces would become extinct. Back then a computer was someone who did really hard maths. Internet was something you shouted at uncooperative fish. URL was what happened if you picked up a stomach bug.

The original Mr Childs can't be blamed, but when *childsexpress.com* was first used in 2003, there was no need for foresight. In fact, someone must have noticed the mistake, because two months later an identical website was set up at *childsbrokerage.com* (known as a mirror site).

So which is the "main" URL? I'm sure they think it's the family-friendly brokerage one, but does the rest of the world see it that way? Fortunately, I have a little test for cases like this: go to Google, search for the company name, and see which one comes out top—that's the one most people will see.

In this case, search for "Childs Express" and Google gives you *childsexpress.com*. Makes me shudder every time.

The Golden Rule

Setting up an online exchange or express is inherently risky, but the rule for avoiding disaster is simple. I've made it easy to remember too, in honour of Childs Express:

Dear Mister Childs to this I profess,

An internet rule for avoiding a mess.

Even a business a hundred years old,

Must move with the times, so go on, be bold!

When naming your website I can't enough stress,

Never precede an exchange (or express) with an "S".

Despite the fact that this particular faux pas has the virtual equivalent of flashing neon signs and a line of showgirls around it, people continue to get caught.

Some, like Experts Exchange, see the light and change their URL. This community of IT professionals could be found at *expertsexchange.com* until June 2004 when they slipped in a hyphen to become *experts-exchange.com*. Easy. One tiny horizontal line was all it took to go from professional gender reassignment to experts swapping stuff.

Others never get the chance to correct their naming blunders. We've seen sex changes that are odd, expert and, um, involve lumberjacks, but all the following exist too:

- *homesexchange.com:* order a DIY kit and reassign your gender in the comfort of your own home.

- *comicsexchange.com:* add killer options to your op like an elbow penis or three boobs. Hilarious!

- *dollarsexchange.com:* where sex changes are cheap as chips (and a battered sausage).

- *studentsexchange.com:* trainee plastic surgeons get real experience and you get a cheap chop, just like getting your barnet trimmed at the hairdressing college.

- *newsexchange.org:* if you didn't like the old one have another attempt here. Like Michael Jackson did with noses.

Sadly, these websites didn't get far off the ground. Their owners must have thought they were great propositions when they bought them, but they have all been allowed to fall into disrepair. They are now parked sites—the internet equivalent of empty houses.

Unoccupied houses attract squatters who, in the absence of a connected water supply, have been known to "visit the bathroom" in any old corner that takes their fancy. Parked sites are similar. But instead of squatters, they attract advertising networks. And instead of crapping just in the corners, they crap advertisements into every available space.

The moral of this story: if you set up an online exchange and don't follow the simple rule, it could end up filled with crap—virtually speaking, of course.

CHAPTER TWO

Apple Pie America

T he Slurls in this section come from small-town America, and display a wholesome naivety that is both touching and worthy of merciless ridicule. It's a culture where lack of cynicism is rife. Some would call it lack of contact with reality.

For example, is there anything wrong with beauty pageants for eight-year old girls, where they are dressed and made-up like adult women and pose provocatively for photos? To me, that's pretty creepy. To others, it's a great way to boost self-esteem and show that every child is beautiful in their own way. Yeah, right. If they're hideously ugly children (hey, it happens) they'd have to be beautiful in an hideously ugly way, and that doesn't really make a lot of sense.*

These Slurls are like beauty pageants for children. No really, they are. It should be obvious, to any sane person, that there is something indecent about them. But somehow, it's all happy-happy smiley-smiley time and the plain wrongness of the situation is repressed deep, deep down. When emotions are repressed they find their way out elsewhere, causing untold mental turmoil. Luckily, in the States, you can easily go out and buy an assault rifle to relieve all that tension.

So that's beauty contests for kids, easy access to semi-automatic weapons, and glaringly obvious Slurls. Welcome to the United States of America.

---

* You might say "but they're beautiful inside!", but they're not. It's all gruesome tubes, organs and blubber in there—really nasty stuff.

Ring of Fire

Premature ejaculation affects between 25% and 40% of American men, so cures for the complaint are big business. Commercial treatments include exercise plans, anaesthetic creams and antidepressants. Sufferers shouldn't discount folk cures, which involve eating green onion seeds, wearing two condoms, or applying Vicks VapoRub to the testicles. The onion seeds probably work by making your breath stink, thereby preventing sex altogether. The condoms and VapoRub approaches are plausible, but don't sound like a lot of fun.

But let's not be too hasty to dismiss the idea of applying menthol goop to your undercarriage—Vicks VapoRub is a salve with many uses. Fans of the ointment smear it on toenail fungus and haemorrhoids, and a Hampshire zoo has even used it to stop meerkats fighting. Honest. The nail fungus myth is so pervasive that the American customer care phone line plays an automated message telling mouldy-toed callers not to use it. And anyone who intentionally applies it to their arsehole should be sectioned immediately.

You might reasonably reject those remedies as old wives' tales, but the problem remains for millions of trigger-happy men. The first step in tackling any issue is to define it accurately—to know your enemy. There are many ways to define premature ejaculation: there are objective tests such as lasting less than two minutes, and subjective ones such as whether the emotional well-being of either partner is adversely affected.

But to put it simply, what we are really talking about is:

`www.cummingfirst.com`

Which, surprisingly, is the website of The First United Methodist Church of Cumming. Despite the name, it's not a chapel for praying to porn stars; it's a local church in Cumming, a town in Georgia, USA.

Misfiring visitors seeking a cure will be disappointed by *cummingfirst.com*—it offers no treatments for their condition. But they will find useful topics to help bring them off the boil: bible studies, prayer lists, and feeding the homeless. If you can reach a computer before the point of no return it's not a bad place to go. But if there's a computer that close by, you were probably not having sex with another person.

The First United Methodist Church of Cumming has now moved to cfumcga.com. *No danger there then. But given the Methodist movement's dim view of homosexuality, it's strange that* cummingfirst.com *has become a blog covering gay issues. Those looking for the Church at its old address will be mightily confused.*

Come to a Sticky End

Some places in the world have funny names, and Cumming is just one of them. I have personally driven through Cocks (in Cornwall) and couldn't resist going back for a photo. I haven't visited Anus (Indonesia) or Bollock (Philippines), but they are surely worth a trip, if only for a great reply to the innocuous question "where did you go on holiday?"

But Cumming does distinguish itself, in a way that could only happen in the land that irony forgot—the town has *two* church websites with incredibly rude URLs. The other one is The First Baptist Church of Cumming. You heard me: the Church of Cumming. The Abbey of Orgasm. The Sanctuary of Spunk. My gratitude must go out to them for filling the hole (snigger) left by *cummingfirst.com*, because they can be found at:

`www.firstbaptistcumming.org`

Which sounds like a perverse challenge for horny rednecks to lose their loads in the fastest time possible. An annual competition, fraught with danger and soaked in a two-hundred year history of blood, sweat, tears and, um, other stuff. It's a battle like no other, a fight to become: First Baptist Cumming.

It would make a great fly-on-the-wall documentary. Louis Theroux, where are you when we need you?

Cabin Fever

Most Americans never cross the borders of their own great nation—three-quarters don't even own passports. You could blame that on ignorance and fear of the outside world, or measly holiday allowances from their employers. You could say they have a huge country of their own to explore, so foreign travel is an unnecessary expense. You could even just chalk it up to bloody good luck for the rest of us.

Whatever you think, there's no doubt that the US has a wealth of attractions for holidaymakers. There are mountain ranges, vast lakes, theme parks and bustling cities. A number of popular destinations can be found in the state parks, nature reserves and national forests of Ohio state. And if you need somewhere to stay there, look no further than the country cabins of Old Man's Haven:

www.oldmanshaven.com

Presumably, every cabin comes with a complimentary hairless geriatric.

Old Man's Haven can be found in the heart of Hocking Hills, where everywhere has a vaguely obscene name. There's Hocking Hills itself, which sounds like a low-grade ventriloquist describing the pain in his ribcage following a triple bypass operation. And the Old Man's Haven website helpfully suggests activities like exploring Old Man's Cave, or "riding the Buckeye trail". Sounds tempting! Now where did I put my old man (shaven)?

Crazy Like a Fox

Fox hunting with horse and hound began in England in the sixteenth century. We can only imagine the forerunners attempted before landing on that particular combination of beasts. Perhaps they placed midgets on greyhounds and sent them after mice. Or maybe they tried an all-animal version, like dog-jockeys on pigs trained to root out badgers.

Whatever its early origins, fox hunting developed into the distinctively British activity we recognise today. But it's not *uniquely* British: hunting with dogs is practised all over the world, from Ireland and Italy to Canada and the USA. In fact it's no longer British at all, since the ban in 2004, when countryside toffs travelled to London to protest. Cockneys were treated to an orderly and polite demonstration, with an array of pleasant tweeds on display. Placards proclaimed "It's jolly well not on" and "Look old bean this isn't cricket". Clandestine afternoon tea speakeasies popped up everywhere, and made a fortune.

In America, fox hunting is legal and known as "fox chasing". They don't kill the animal but just enjoy the thrill of the pursuit. A regular hunt may not have a kill for several years, despite chasing several foxes in a single day's hunting. In other words: they scare hundreds of foxes shitless, performing no useful function, and run around and around in circles until the confused animal goes down a burrow. Complete bloody waste of time.

Given this reluctance to harm foxes, it's strange that the official sports website for Marist College in Poughkeepsie, New York, can be found at:

www.goredfoxes.com

Visitors hoping to see Basil Brush with his guts out will be disappointed: despite the name the site does not showcase fox hunting's best-loved mutilations in a twisted marks-out-of-ten slide show.

Why did Marist College choose this particular URL? Well, all US college sports teams have nicknames, and Marist is no exception. Their team is known as the Red Foxes, after their mascot (which is a red fox, dummy). It makes perfect sense, with typical American exuberance, that the official sports website adds "Go!" to their nickname. It's a little more mysterious why they would subject their beloved Foxes to such a public goring.

The Go Red Foxes website is now hosted by American TV network CBS. They didn't take the opportunity to become an ex-Slurl though, as goredfoxes.com *now redirects viewers to* goredfoxes.cstv.com.

Sunday Monday Happy Gays

There's something endearing about a "Big Al". Maybe it's down to Al Delvecchio from Happy Days, played by the lovely Al Molinaro. In real life he went on to open a chain of diners in the American Midwest, and he called it "Big Al's".* Now that's endearing.

Many businesses have capitalized on the cuddliness of a Big Al. There's Big Al's Bar, Big Al's Limos, Big Al's Barbershop, Big Al's Pizza, even Big Al's Bouncy Castles. Get Big Al in your name and you immediately generate feelings of nostalgia, sentimentality, even love. So when Big Al's Bowling Alley (in Washington State) wanted a website, the choice of name was obvious:

`www.ilovebigals.com`

Making site visitors type "I love" to get to your web site is bound to inspire doe-eyed devotion, so throw it in there by all means. We all love bi gals on the internet.

Big Al's is so successful, the Kirkwood family of Vancouver is building a second location. Where have they chosen to begin their expansion? Beaverton, Oregon. Of course.

---

* Don't get confused here: the diner in Happy Days wasn't called Big Al's, it was called Arnold's Drive-In. I'd hate for you to embarrass yourself next time it comes up in conversation.

If That's True I'll Eat My Hat Block

There are many mysteries in this world, but the art of traditional hat-making is one that few people concern themselves with. Let's fly in the face of convention and take a look at it anyway. So, how does a hatter make a hat? Well, they build it around a wooden block carved into the shape of a hat—that's the secret.

Now, if I know anything at all about trees it's that they don't grow naturally into hat-shaped lumps, so where do hat makers get their hat blocks from? Believe it or not, there is a second profession involved in hat making—that of the block shaper. These craftsmen do nothing but carve solid wooden hats of every style and size—an activity which appears to be complete lunacy if you don't know the secret of their purpose. It isn't a hugely popular profession, but you can still find a few talented block shapers online. One such craftsman is Fred Raab of Beverly, New Jersey, who you can find at:

www.fredshatblocks.com

No, don't be silly, Fred hasn't been eating his blocks. They're hat blocks, and they're Fred's: Fred's Hat Blocks. Some say apostrophes are outdated, but if you want to possess blocks rather than produce them they make all the difference.

Pumping Iron

American Scrap Metal is a scrap metal recycling company based in Fort Worth, Texas.

www.americanscrapmetal.com

We can learn something here from *Team America: World Police*. The movie offers great insights into the culture of the United States, distilling their go-getting nature into just three words:

America, fuck yeah!

That's the kind of inspiring Yankee spirit that goes into an endeavour like Americans Crap Metal. Only a true doodle dandy would deliberately swallow a case of brass handles, for the patriotic honour of straining blue-faced over the potty for five hours. Americans crap metal, wooh yeah!*

The site shows an impressive range of metals previously crapped by gung-ho star-spangled-banner-botherers. These include, um, a cog thing, nuts and bolts, copper wire, mesh stuff . . . basically loads of crazy metal, OK? Not only does Americans

---

* Americans don't just crap metal—they also sneeze lightning, belch fireballs and piss molten rock. Lord knows what their other bodily functions produce.

Crap Metal promote this great pastime, it will even subsidise your efforts:

"We will inspect your material on site and quote you a price"

What a fantastic opportunity! A whole generation of Texans missed the oil bonanza, but now there's a new way to get rich quick: brown gold. There's no need to dig wells or build refineries, just rummage around for old paperclips and bent nails, and scoff them down. Then get down to Americans Crap Metal and produce your new "material" for inspection. It's money for old rope (but with a much better price for old chain).

Pass the Senokot

Did you know that, in the US, scrapbook making is more popular than golf? One in five households have someone who plays golf, but one in four has a scrapbooking enthusiast. And the scrapbook industry is huge, with six thousand stores selling $2.5 billion of supplies in a year.

The hobby is dominated by women with families, but they're not the only ones to indulge: when *Creating Keepsakes* magazine ran a Hall of Fame competition one winner was Mitchell Kraft, an eighteen year-old university student from Minnesota. I'm sure he received hearty slaps on the back from his fraternity buddies, and had to bat away droves of young college girls made horny by his triumph. And rightly so. If sticking baby teeth and bits of coloured tissue paper into a photo album isn't cool, then for heaven's sake what is?

Despite its homely feel, scrapbooking can be an expensive pastime. Not only that, good results require nimble fingers, intense concentration, and many hours of effort. But one website has the answer for stingy ham-fisted scrapbookers who can't sit still for five minutes (I admit that is a slight paraphrasing of their marketing message). The solution is digital scrapbooking, using pre-built templates from:

www.1hourscrap.com

So say goodbye to all the mess and strain you've had with previous efforts; sit down, relax, and produce a perfectly formed specimen in only one hour.

To be honest, it still sounds like a long time to me. If it takes that long I suggest you lay off the huge steaks and stock up on fresh fruit and vegetables. It's not normal, one hour's crap.

An hour's crap is impressive, but it's nothing compared to scrapbook supplies company www.oneworldscrap.com. This multilingual website offers a shop, gallery and forum, truly straddling the global scrapbooking community. Or should that be squatting over?

Paint it Pink

Homophobia is all too common in the States. It's subtly expressed in urban myths about celebrities caught in bizarre sexual acts, or prominent organisations secretly promoting homosexuality. Somehow, it's easier for Americans to believe wacky stories than the banal truth.

Legends of the first variety—celebrities caught red-handed with everything but the kitchen sink up their bottoms—include tales like Richard Gere being admitted to hospital with a gerbil stuck up his bum, requiring an emergency gerbilectomy. Another is the notorious story that Marc Almond collapsed and had to have his stomach pumped to remove a gallon of semen.*

Actually, those stories are complete fiction. The claims don't even begin to stack up: there are no recorded cases of "gerbilling" *ever*, no-one's stomach can hold a gallon, and semen isn't toxic. But never mind.

Rumours of the second type—ominous conspiracies to turn straights into gays with subliminal messages—include the idea that clothes shop The Gap was founded by homosexuals who derived its name from "Gay and Proud". In truth, The Gap was founded by a husband-and-wife couple and the name refers to "the generation gap", a popular term when the business was founded in 1969.

---

* This story has been attributed to over a dozen different celebrities, including Britney Spears and The Bay City Rollers. Shang-A-Lang indeed.

Another invention is that *Sesame Street's* Bert and Ernie are gay and a forthcoming episode will feature their marriage. Granted, if Bert and Ernie were human adult men then their behaviour would seem a bit fruity. But they're actually children's puppets of an indeterminate species with odd-shaped heads—and the program's makers have confirmed that they don't portray a gay couple.

Now there's a new pink peril, and it's the greatest threat against straight-hood ever known: the Fag Ray. From miles away cackling queens can target heterosexuals with this weapon of ass destruction, and zap them into limp-wristed Kylie fans forever. The secret gay coalition behind this atrocity are so bold that they even have a website for it:

`www.fagray.com`

Sure, it says it's the home of F.A. Gray, the largest painting contractor in New Hampshire, but that's obviously a cover story. The time has come for vigilance. Keep your back to the wall and your eyes peeled, and if you drop the soap don't even *think* about picking it up. The Fag Ray is coming.

Water Into Wine

Ingleside Vineyards is a winery located in the "Northern Neck" region of Virginia.

www.ipwine.com

It's good of them to spell out just how they produce their booze. While other vineyards are messing with big vats and tricky things like fermentation, Ingleside just feed the grapes to a messiah-like figure whose kidneys transform it to fine plonk which is urinated straight into the bottle. Cork in, label on, and you're done. The poor fella must have indigestion though: Ingleside produces thousands of bottles of wine in eighteen different varieties.

Why did they chose *ipwine.com* as their address? Well, IP means "Internet Protocol"—the network technology used on the internet. There was a trend at one point of calling anything internet related IP-this and IP-that, so that might explain it. It seems ridiculous now. I think somebody noticed and we lost gems such as *ipanywhere.com* (software for accessing your computer remotely). Thank heavens we still have *ipwine.com* to hang onto.* Sniff.

---

* There's also *ipallover.no*, which suggests a drunken disaster followed swiftly by regret. But it's a bit unfair to giggle, seeing as they're Norwegian.

Lights, Camera, Paintbrush

Action Paintball Games is a paintball park located in the city of Sacramento, California.

www.actionpaintballsac.com

It's a classic case. A logical approach to website naming has resulted in an URL that sounds like a challenge in one of those extreme Japanese game shows. Or Steven Spielberg instructing an actor to daub his testicles with a few coats of Tuscan Terracotta.

What's so logical about this domain name anyway? Well, let's think about it. What would have been the *best* name for them? I'd have to say *paintball.com*, but that was registered in 1996, so it wasn't an option. Second choice would be *actionpaintball.com* but that went to an Aussie venue of the same name in 1997. Anyway, it's important to get across where the park is located, so it makes perfect sense to think about *actionpaintballsacramento.com*. No, that's way too long.

Fortunately, Sacramento has an abbreviation used by the county's executive airport and loads of local websites: Sac. The thing is, the Sacramento zoo, ballet, library, and opera can all display their Sacs with impunity, but as soon as balls are involved (even ones filled with paint) it's a completely different story.

Some philistines use the spelling "ball sack" (with a K) but "sac" is the proper biological term for the scrotum—and any other fleshy pouches you may have attached to your body.

Ask a Silly Question . . .

Aptronyms are names which are perfectly suited to their owners. For example, a 1977 study of incontinence surgery was authored by A.J. Splatt and D. Weedon. If you don't believe me, check out volume 49 of the British Journal of Urology, pages 173–176.

Another example: the University of Rhode Island's oceanography program was started way back by Dr Charles Fish, who hired Saul B. Saila, who years later saw the department headed up by Dean Jeff Seemann. And Wolfgang Wolf was a former manager of German football club VFL Wolfsburg. Now that's just silly.

There is a school of thought, called nominative determinism, that aptronyms are more than mere coincidence; that we are influenced by our names and gravitate to professions which match. A famous example is Thomas Crapper, inventor of the ballcock and other lavatorial advances. Contrary to popular belief, the verb "to crap" does not come from Mr Crapper—people have been crapping since the fifteenth century. At least.

Here's one last wonderfully appropriate example of nominative determinism:

www.amigonefuneralhome.com

Amigone Funeral Home was founded by Daniel D. Amigone in 1926, and today serves Western New York state with its fourteen funeral home locations.

So if you wake up on a cold hard slab, naked and surrounded by coffins, you might well ask "Where am I? Is this really happening? Am I gone? *Am I gone?*" If you can ask that question then you really shouldn't be there. But if an undertaker replies "That's my name, don't wear it out," take comfort in knowing roughly where you are: Western New York state, maybe down Buffalo way. Still, you better get out of there before he injects you with embalming fluid and sucks your guts out.

CHAPTER THREE

In Good Company

T he websites in this chapter are the corporate world's contributions to the Slurls gene pool. Big corporations are known for spending millions on "re-branding" and making a big balls-up of it. For example, in 2002 accounting firm PWC renamed its consulting division "Monday". By the time employees, clients and competitors had stopped laughing the whole thing was sold to IBM, who promptly killed off the silly name.

The cost? An estimated £75 million. The logic? Everybody loves Mondays and leaps out of bed before the alarm goes off, bounding with energy and misty eyed with joy at the challenges of the week ahead—thank God that horrible weekend is over! Never mind that Monday is the most common day for suicides and heart attacks. Don't pay any attention to the chart-topping song about a real-life Monday massacre, which the murderess explained with "I don't like Mondays. This livens up the day." Oh no, we all love Mondays.

PWC went wrong when they asked the only person in the world who likes the first day of the working week to think up a new name for them. How about the other firms in this chapter— what's their excuse? Again, I think we must lay the blame on branding—the idea that you can make a name mean anything you want it to. I'm sure that's true in some cases, where the words aren't already meaningful and you have plenty of time and money.

But there's only so much you can achieve. After all, you can't polish a turd. Or for the squeamish: you can't make a silk purse out of a sow's ear. Actually, stitching together bits of pig is almost as grisly as buffing up poo. And maybe that's a hint at the problem—people in business have become too squeamish, too scared of causing offence, to speak the truth when an awful brand name is proposed. Like the fawning lackeys in *The Emperor's New Clothes*, no-one has the nerve to protest when the company wanders around with its balls on display.

Anyway, the corporate world is so full of jargon, even those with the courage and common sense to speak out often fail to wrangle their thoughts into business-friendly language. The senior director of marketing might chuckle, and recommend they all sing from the same hymn sheet. He thinks he's made his point. The branding consulting nods sagely and mumbles something about deliverables. Now they think they've got their ducks in a row. They haven't. A couple of ducks are bobbing away happily, but most caught mange and all their feathers fell out. Another was eaten by a dog, and half the new chicks drowned weeks ago when a boy ran them over with a remote-control model of the QE2. Meanwhile, the only song on the hymn sheet is Agadoo, scratched on with a biro stolen from Argos. Oblivious, the company carries on rowing up shit creek, frantically polishing the turds floating past.

If businesses could give up their waffle and talk a little sense, they could probably avoid the naming disasters in this chapter. But where's the fun in that for us?

Mofos and Proud Of It

The law firm of Morrison & Foerster has more than a thousand lawyers in seventeen offices around the world. In their own immodest words, the firm has "unsurpassed expertise in finance, life sciences, and technology, legendary litigation skills, and an unrivalled reach across the Pacific Rim." Promising law school students with an interest in Asian culture should contact them post-haste about the possibility of a Pacific Rim job.

Morrison & Foerster have a good claim to the first ever Slurl, having registered their domain name in October 1992:

www.mofo.com

They are also unusual because MoFo has been their official abbreviation since 1973, and is widely used in the industry. But MoFo is more than just a nickname: they have actually played up to it, naming website pages "MoFo Overview", "MoFo Offices", and "MoFo Careers" like a foul-mouthed gangster rapper who can't string two words together without an expletive. Only lawyers could be pleased with an incestuous nickname.

Yet they have managed to avoid widespread ridicule. Why is that? Simple—they're lawyers. Pointing out that lawyers are mofos is no more controversial than saying computer programmers lack personal hygiene skills or glamour models are not very bright—it's just a fact of life.

III Communication

The O'Neill Building is a glorious art deco landmark on Sixth Avenue in New York City. Built in 1887 and taking up a whole block, it was a fashion emporium on what was then called "The Ladies' Mile". It is now owned by El-Ad Properties, a cash-rich company that will happily spend a billion dollars on some land and another billion building something nice on it. For breakfast.

Judging by its URL, the O'Neill Building has come down with a case of SBS—sick building syndrome—a combination of seemingly unrelated ailments caused by poor air quality:

```
www.theoneillbuilding.com
```

SBS is recognised as a disorder in a report by the WHO (the World Health Organisation, not the rock group—I doubt they could give a toss about it). The owner of a sick building may experience high levels of absenteeism, low productivity, poor job satisfaction and high employee turnover. Another explanation for that could be crap pay, dull work, and shit-for-brains management, but—oh yes—SBS is a much more likely culprit.

Then again, maybe the building is ill in a Beastie Boys kind of way—it is in New York after all. Don't know what "ill" means as a slang term? Well, at the Urban Dictionary, everyone can (and does) contribute to a collection of over 3 million slang definitions. "Ill" is helpfully defined as cool or crazy, in the main part. But Urban Dictionary's sub-normal contributors have also defined it as "sumthin datz madd hot", "pulling the crud", and "totaly awesome pimpatude". Thank God that's been cleared up.

Ball Busters

Go Red For Women is a campaign run by the American Heart Association to educate women about heart disease and stroke. The colour red and a red dress logo are campaign themes.

www.goredforwomen.com

I'm all for charities that spell out the dangers of scoffing deep-fried bacon double-cheeseburgers, avoiding exercise, and smoking like it's going out of fashion (too late, it already has).

But what's with all the goring? Does campaign figurehead Andie MacDowell keep the sworn enemies of human females—men—shackled in her Hollywood mansion's underground car park? Are they kept awake for days on end, starved, and whipped into a rage by repeated jabs from the sharp corners of Andie's unfeasibly square jaw? Of course they are.

The night before every sponsored bake-off, bra-burning, and shop-a-thon, supporters congregate at Andie's pad in their jimmy-jams for a spot of illegal man-fighting. Now as every woman knows, men are base creatures, ruled by their animal instincts for sex, violence, and pastry filled with meat and gravy. After a few days of firm treatment they are baying for each others' blood.

The ladies form a circle and release two grunting brutes. Having been starved of pie they go straight for the fleshy, vulnerable areas and tear off chunks with their vicious incisors and sharpened copies of Loaded. All the time the cruel spectators place bets, shout encouragement, file their nails, and do a little light crochet. It's a nasty business, being gored for women.

Just like goredfoxes.com *earlier, this URL suffers from its blind enthusiasm for a cause. It could never be a problem in the real world, but online there's no difference between shouting "go red!" and "gored!"*

That's Rubbish

Computers and other electronic products become obsolete very quickly. Take a new laptop for example, you might get three years out of it before buying a new model. If you have an unusually high ridicule threshold you might make it to five before the embarrassment becomes too much to bear. For a mobile phone, it's a year max before your ego collapses under the sheer weight of peer pressure.

Some people take pride in ignoring the rest of civilisation but even they upgrade in the end, whether they like it or not, because obsolescence is an integral part of the computer business. For example, you may be happy plugging away on Windows 98, but really need a cheap little program that only runs on Windows XP, which in turn won't run on your cranky old machine.

So you pop to PC World to pick up a cheap replacement, but get seduced by flashing lights, skinny screens and shiny plastic—oh God it's so shiny. Suddenly you understand: you can stick with the drudgery of your boring old life, or splash out and become the talk of the town. Instead of nights on your own in the corner of the pub, you'll hold court at the bar, confidently reciting facts about your beautiful shiny (so shiny) new plastic friend. Who could resist? In a dreamy haze you produce a credit card and enter your PIN. You don't know how to stop yourself. An instant later buyer's remorse sets in, as you realise a twenty quid program just cost you a grand.

But what happens to all those old electronics, which were so beloved until moments before their replacement? Well, you might toss them nonchalantly into the bin, but like so much of the waste we produce today, they should be recycled. Yes, yet another thing we are supposed to recycle via an ever-growing collection of bins, boxes, prepaid envelopes and trips to the rubbish tip. For most people recycling is a drag, but for others— the companies who process the stuff—it's fantastic.

So it's a good time to be in the recycling business, and a boom time if, like Regency Technologies of Solon, Ohio, you specialise in scrap IT. You can find Regency Technologies at:

www.itscrap.com

Yes, that's right: IT Scrap. They take old computers and fix them up or crunch them to bits, depending on age. That's true recycling, getting something of value out of stuff that no-one wants. The URL says it's crap, but I think it's great.

Pool Party Pooper

There is no bigger social faux pas than taking a dump in a swimming pool. People really don't like it. And it's not just poor etiquette, it's dirty too. The American Centre for Disease Control (CDC) recommends closing a public pool for half an hour after a "formed stool" episode and a full day following a "diarrheal incident". Detailed guidelines and charts are included in the CDC's sober educational pamphlet "Fecal Incident Response Recommendations"—it's an interesting read but probably not worthy of the Nobel prize for literature.

Attitudes do differ however. In 2008 staff at a public swimming pool in Scotland responded to a solid dump in the deep end by nonchalantly fishing the item out, while families continued swimming and playing around them. Let's hope they were careful when they scooped it up: I can just imagine them chasing a big log back and forth across the pool, swimmers desperately doggy-paddling away, while the turd follows them on a roll of surf.

Scottish indifference aside, it's generally accepted that pool hygiene is important. The water is normally disinfected using expensive machinery and chemicals—taking up a large chunk of maintenance costs. One supplier of swimming pool cleaning products is Connecticut company Arch Chemicals, with their POOLIFE brand:

```
www.poolife.com
```

Well done Arch Chemicals. You have successfully tied the image of a sparkly clean swimming pool with the absolute opposite: having a big old poo floating in the shallow end.

Arch Chemicals stopped using poolife.com *in 2005 and now it's just a shortcut to* archchemicals.com. *But the POOLIFE name lives on, and is splattered liberally all over the new site and their products. Why is it, when they happily keep the double "ch" in* archchemicals.com, *that they can't see the advantage to a double L in POOLIFE?*

Tissues and Issues

SCA is a $13 billion multinational that produces and sells absorbent hygiene products, packaging solutions and "publication papers"—whatever the hell *they* are.

www.scatissue.com

You might not be familiar with scat. It's a word of many meanings, from a command to trespassing cats to irritating jazz singing (skip-a-be-doo-dop-be-diddle-cock-doobie—you get the idea). It's also slang for whisky and even heroin, but the most apt meaning here is animal dung. Who doesn't have an issue with that?

Me Tarzan You Jim

They are close to anonymity in the UK, but the Wendy's chain of fast food restaurants is a household name in the US, just behind McDonalds and Burger King. Its signature is square beef burgers because, we are told, they "don't cut corners".

The first interesting thing about Wendy's is that it isn't Wendy's at all, it's Dave's—the chain was founded by Dave Thomas of Bellville, New Jersey in 1969. The second interesting thing is that Dave named his new burger bar after his daughter, Melinda. Now, I can imagine daddy Dave bumbling around naming restaurants after non-existent children, but Wendy was actually a nickname given to Melinda by her siblings. Well, that's the official line; with a family of five it's forgivable to forget what the hell you called them all.

Wendy's is a responsible company, and gives back to society with the catchily-named Wendy's High School Heisman Memorial Trophy Award, a scheme that has celebrated excellence in athletics, academics and the community since 1994. The program is often shortened to Wendy's High School Heisman, but even that's too long for the website, which squeezes it way down to:

www.wendysheisman.com

So to summarise: Wendy's is Dave's, who named it after Melinda. Who, if we believe the URL, is a man. If I was her, I'd hide my secret better.

What is Art?

Humans have contemplated the nature of art ever since Ug and Og painted cave walls in southern France around 16,000 years ago. Here's how it began:

"This art. Me artist." said Ug, proudly presenting his lifelike daubing of a huge black bull.

"No Ug. That not art. Me make art." replied Og, indicating his abstract designs with a flourish.

"Og, me think you pretentious wanker." said Ug, while clubbing Og to death. Og's demise caused the resale value of his work to skyrocket, but everyone ridiculed Ug's output—even the low-brow Neanderthals. So Ug clubbed the Neanderthals to death.

Art critics have continued the debate in a similar manner ever since. But with a little less clubbing.

In 1897 Leo Tolstoy threw his hat into the ring, with his book *What is Art?* In this seminal work, Tolstoy rejected theories which define art by its goodness, truth or beauty, and instead put forward the idea that art is the effective communication of emotion. Tolstoy thought nursery rhymes had greater artistic merit than Beethoven's symphonies, because the composer's efforts were too brainy and emotionless. A direct

---

* Translated from the original French

line can be drawn between Tolstoy's ideas and today's convention of calling every hysterical warbling anorexic that stumbles into the pop charts an artist. Thanks for that Leo.

So really, what is art? A concept this complex cannot be explained literally; we must use metaphor to understand it. Art could be an eagle that soars effortlessly above us. Or a dream that cannot be grasped through force, only experienced firsthand. Perhaps art is the very soul of our culture?

Yeah, maybe. But someone knows the metaphor that truly explains art: New York company American Home Food Product Incorporated. One of its subsidiaries is Artisanal Premium Cheese, an online shop selling a range of two hundred handcrafted cheeses from around the world.

www.artisanalcheese.com

That's right: art is anal cheese. I can't tell you how and why art is anal cheese, or even what anal cheese is, but if you like "stinky cheeses" (as Artisanal delightfully calls them) then it surely sounds delicious!

Anyway, all this cheese talk has made me hungry. Now, where on earth did I put the Stinking Bishop?

CHAPTER FOUR

It's Not Rocket Surgery

L et's take a look at science and technology. You might expect the kind of brain-boxes who study the universe, program computers and design websites to nimbly avoid the pitfalls that would saddle them with a Slurl. Not so. In fact, their techie nature seems to produce a blindness to even obvious double meanings.

Take *therapistfinder.com* for example—what do you see in that at first glance? The rapist finder? Thought so. It's a desperate situation when the unintended meaning is easier to spot than the intended one. Most techie Slurls are like that; warty beasts which only a mother could find easy on the eye.

Why is this? Maybe it's because there's a lot of jargon in computing, and techies quickly learn definitions that don't agree with the dictionary. For example: ten years ago "spyware" meant a pair of sunglasses, trilby hat and an overcoat; now it means a program that takes over your computer. "Backwards-compatible" meant something even an idiot could use, now it means that your favourite programs don't work anymore and you have to give Bill Gates even more money. "Megahertz" was what you felt after a kick in the balls, now, er . . . look, nobody knows what it means, it was just made up to sell us computers.

When geeks aren't selling us stuff that we didn't know we needed they're setting up websites. With the language centre of their brains squashed into a corner by techno-jargon, Star Trek trivia, and Natalie Portman* fantasies, they sometimes get their URLs in a twist. These sites are a few of the end results.

---

* At a whisker past jailbait, Miss Portman played Queen Amidala in the new (meaning "awful") Star Wars films. Geeks worldwide dropped their Doritos when she appeared in blue face paint and a costume modelled on Mongolian imperial fashion—the nerd equivalent of a tan and a skimpy swimming costume.

Agent Provocateur

Who Represents? has been providing contact information for celebrities and their agents since 2001. For $12.99 per month you can search their database up to one hundred times in a day, so all but really hardcore stalkers should be satisfied.

www.whorepresents.com

That's all well and good but I think they could do much better with that name. They could sell prostitute-themed giftware. Or gifts *for* prostitutes. Or gifts *of* prostitutes. The possibilities are endless, but the whore-token idea has real legs. We already have book tokens, bestowed nationwide in acts of apathetic generosity, avoiding any use of the imagination, and forcing the recipient to read a whole bloody bunch of words.*

So why not Whore Tokens? Slut Vouchers? Tart Coupons? Forget bungee jumping, many a teenage boy would be delighted to tear open an envelope from Red Letter Days to find one of those "experiences" inside.

---

* The one time it's reasonable to read words is on the toilet.

Leopard-Compatible CocoaSuite

Bit Art Consulting is a small American computer programming firm, specializing in communication, publishing and manufacturing systems. They are particularly skilled in "hybrid applications".

www.bitart.com

There's more to Bit Art than an URL which sounds like the blog of a bisexual bimbo: it's a veritable haven for silly names. The company actually writes its name as BITart, shouting its misnomer at you. It's based in Minnetonka, Minnesota. It's run by Gerd Knops.

The company's main technology specialism is stuff-that-isn't-Microsoft. One benefit for advocates of stuff-that-isn't-Microsoft is the entitlement to adopt an air of smug superiority. Another perk is running together sentences that are nonsensical to anybody who isn't in their dull little club. For example, Bit Art scream with glee about their latest software, calling it . . .

Leopard-compatible CocoaSuite

Sounds delicious. What else have they got? Koala-compatible lemon bonbons? A banoffee pie that is pleasing to hamsters? Scotch pancakes that your pet chinchilla will like?

You knew where you were when programs had names like WordPerfect 10.2 and VisiCalc 4.0. Now it's all desserts and animals. For example, Apple uses a series of big cat names for versions of its operating system OS X—starting with Cheetah, then taking in Puma, Jaguar, Panther, Tiger, Leopard and Snow Leopard. How wonderfully furry and charming. But they're swiftly using up the sexy cat species and won't look so clever when they reach version Ocelot.

Apple have avoided cutesy names with the wildly successful iPhone. The latest iteration is dubbed the 3GS, named after the third-generation mobile phone network plus an S for "speed". But they have more than just swiftness to boast about—the iPhone's innovations have redefined the mobile phone market. One important advance is a technology which enables the touch-sensitive screen to detect movements involving more than one finger, known as "multi-touch".

Multi-touch enables the use of intuitive screen "gestures", such as the pervy-sounding Pinch and Spread. In fact, many iPhone gestures both look and sound sexual. When users aren't spreading their fingers to zoom in, or pinching to zoom out, they are sliding to scroll slowly and flicking to scroll quickly. I suspect a ploy to encourage them to develop an erotic relationship with the glossy black device. And when they do, there's an application called MyVibe which turns it into a vibrator. No kidding.

Rodent Banquet

A while back rating sites were all the rage. The biggest site—Am I Hot or Not—launched in 2000, and was one of the most popular websites in the world for a time. It was sold recently for a rumoured $20 million, but no doubt could have fetched several zillion at the height of the dot-com boom.

The concept of rating sites is simple but addictive—you rate the attractiveness of photographs from 1 to 10. They're a great way to kill time whilst barely having to think, on a scale surpassed only by daytime television.

There is a scientific explanation for the instinctive appeal of rating sites. A 2006 study at the Washington University School of Medicine concluded that a basic function of the brain is to classify images into hot or not—and this can be done subconsciously long before the viewer is aware they are seeing the picture. Armed with this knowledge, I can see a future where babies are not only encouraged to develop language and motor skills,* but also plied with back copies of Heat magazine to hone the crucial "hot or not" area of the brain, which will be dubbed the fittocampus.

Different spins on the rating site idea include rating the cuteness of pets and the competence of police officers, and there's even a site called Rate My Poo. Don't be tempted to visit the last site—you will regret it. If that tempts you to visit it all the

---

* So they can fix our cars.

more, then I insist that you do visit it (reverse psychology—works every time).

Rate-a-Ten has an angle all of its own: you can rate Guys, Girls, and "Other Types". The first two categories I am familiar with, but what the hell are Other Types? Pictures of people half-eaten by rats? That would fit the site's name and—if you ask me—be slightly preferable to rating poo.

www.rateaten.com

Sadly, Rate-a-Ten have gone out of business. Who could have predicted that?

Where The Sun Don't Shine

This one's a little unfair, because it's actually a single real word. But if you told someone you were looking at analemma videos on the internet, would they think you meant examples of an astronomical phenomenon or nasty butt-porn featuring a Jane Austen heroine?

Here's the website of the Analemma Society (yes, a whole society), based in Great Falls, Virginia:

```
www.analemma.org
```

So what is an analemma anyway? Well, if you plot the position of the sun at the same time of day, every day for a year, you will have traced out a nice figure-of-eight shape—that's an analemma. Completely pointless, and a good indication that you have got far too much time on your hands. Get a job, you work-shy fop.

Beyond Therapy

Therapist Finder is a directory of nearly 8,000 licensed mental health professionals in California.

www.therapistfinder.com

The word "therapist" has always required a certain amount of care. Before the internet, the main risk was bad printing or sloppy sign writing: use all-capitals and a little extra spacing between letters and it's goodbye therapist, hi there to your friendly neighbourhood rapist. Gasps all round.

The problem achieves a completely different scale on the internet. Here's a few more in the same vein:

sydneytherapist.com

An Australian counsellor. Or a website belonging to Sydney, who just can't stop blogging about his nasty little hobby.

therapistschoice.com

Medical supplies shop. They could branch out into Rohypnol. And maybe duct tape.

therapistinabox.com

This site sells CD box-sets of Do It Yourself psychotherapy. It could have hired out big boxes in the shape of birthday cakes—like the ones which conceal scantily-clad bunny girls. At the perfect moment, out jumps . . . a rapist. Surprise! It will be.

As Brown as a Berry

Research in Motion (RIM) is the company behind the Black-Berry mobile phone, a gadget renowned for making email accessible on the move. In fact, the original BlackBerrys *only* did email.

As a growing young business RIM are always on the look out for good people. The careers section of their website can be found at *rim.com/careers*, or via it's own dedicated shortcut:

```
www.rim.jobs
```

New graduates with an enthusiastic interest in RIM jobs can apply for newly opened positions in a fast-paced environment, with hands-on training. After their lazy student days, that should see them licked swiftly into shape.

As long as there's a company called RIM, there's fun to be had guffawing at the idea of being employed by them. For example: in 2008 competitor Motorola announced job cuts and blocked RIM from hiring their redundant workers, using an agreement they had made not to solicit each others employees. It was widely reported in the business press, but they all missed the obvious headline: "Motorola Stops Laid Off Workers Getting RIM Jobs". Exotic sexual acts might not be everybody's post-redundancy pick-me-up, but there's no accounting for taste. As in preference, not flavour.

rim.jobs *isn't a true Slurl because it's a shortcut rather than a website in its own right, but it stands out for sheer economy of space—not one character is wasted.*

The Good, the Bad, and the Spotty

The *Black Hat SEO eBook* is a downloadable book about improving your website's position in search engine results.

www.blackhatebook.com

I doubt the site is successful, as the target audience seems to be the small minority of racists who can actually read.

Before the site's author is murdered (or bombarded with invites to Ku Klux Klan rallies) I should point out that there really is something called Black Hat SEO. Let me explain: a black hat is worn by the villain in cowboy films, and SEO stands for Search Engine Optimisation, so Black Hat SEO is using villainous methods to improve your search engine ranking. Yes, really. It's a ridiculously romantic term for spotty adolescents fiddling with computers in darkened rooms smelling of beef and onion flavour crisps.

Black Hat SEO practitioners play a cat-and-mouse game with the search engines—as one devious method is detected and offending pages banned, another is devised to take its place. Techniques currently in use have mysterious Harry Potter-esque names like *cloaking* (showing a different version of a page to search engines) and *doorway pages* (tricking users into seeing pages they didn't intend to visit). So far, so naughty—their parents should give 'em a ruddy good clip around the ear.

But there's more. *Negative SEO* gets a competitor's website banned from the search engines by deliberately promoting them with outdated (and therefore banned) Black Hat methods, or simply grassing them up for their own minor transgressions. *Page hijacking* is creating a copy of a popular web page, such as a bank or online shop, and completely replacing it in the search results, so people mistake the fake version for the genuine site. That goes way beyond naughty cowboys and Indians. Maybe it's time to drum up a posse and head out for some good old-fashioned black hat lynching.

A New Breed of Juvenile Humour

Analtech Inc., of Delaware, work in the area of thin layer chromatography, a technique used to monitor reactions in chemistry labs.

www.analtech.com

The Analtech name might be OK for a company at the cutting edge of rectal thermometer design, but everyone else should keep well away.

You've got to feel sorry for Analtech: they were established back in 1961 as Custom Service Chemicals, and acquired their current name three years later on the recommendation of a marketing firm, who advised them:

Well, you guys do Analytical Technology—why don't you put the two words together and call it "Analtech"?

Why indeed. The correct response to the marketer's question was "because that's a bloody awful name!" But no, Custom Service Chemicals jumped right in.

In January 2009 the company sent a questionnaire to customers asking if they should change their name. The despondent email explained that Analtech was respected worldwide by the scientific community, and their brand name should be a huge success after nearly 50 years of use, but that a new breed of juvenile humour had developed "in the past few decades" and—worse still—web filters were blocking the company's name. If this new humour (which I can't possibly condone) has been around for that long, shouldn't they have done something about it a bit sooner? Besides, I suspect juvenile humour has been around for a few millennia, not just a few decades: didn't the Romans enjoy willy and bum gags?

Anyway, it sounds like Analtech have finally come to their senses, and I'm happy to help out in the search for a new name. I think the perfect name would be Analytical Resources for Scientific Experiments and Technology, or ArseTech for short.

Bum Buddies

ARS eCommerce is a web design and internet marketing agency with offices in three US states.

www.arsecommerce.com

This URL maintains the computer industry tradition of blindly ignoring what's right in front of your nose: an arse, in this case. When ARS aren't batting away enquiries from people who think they're an agency for rent boys, perhaps they go out for coffee with other bum-fixated companies, like Analtech.

In 2008 ARS moved to thinkars.com, very nearly winning them the honour of being the only company to change from one Slurl to another. A slogan they market themselves with is "Think Bold. Think Smart. Think ARS."—a unique campaign to associate computer services with a big old pair of butt cheeks. Advertising can sell sanitary towels with roller skating* so it might just work.

---

* You know, in the advert: "Waaaaaaaaah, Body Form!"

I Got Three Problems and a Wombat Ain't One

WOMbeat is a local business recommendation website, so you can rate your builder and review restaurants. Its tagline is "Word Of Mouth . . . Only Better!"

www.wombeat.com

There are three problems here. The first problem is that nobody—other than marketing wonks—has ever heard of the acronym WOM (word of mouth). The second problem is that everybody knows what a "womb" is and what "eat" means. The third problem is that putting those two words together doesn't paint a pretty picture.

Womb eating may not be in the best taste (literally) but it's not unheard of for people to eat placenta. They reckon that mums who munch their afterbirth have a reduced risk of post-natal depression, but there is no proof for the theory. I can explain it though: if you eat your placenta you are already mental, and a little bit of baby blues won't register over the maniacal laughter and little pink fairies going wee wee wee.

The WOMbeat logo features a cartoon wombat giving the thumbs-up sign. WOMbeat—wombat, geddit? The use of a wombat explains everything, because the Aussie mammals are well known for, um, digging burrows and having perfectly cubic poo.* Maybe they are also great for recommending plumbers, but it hasn't come up in the scientific literature.

* Nineteenth-century bushmen wrote numbers on all six sides of wombat poos and used them as dice. It's true!

Go-Go Gadget

Some people just love their gadgets. You can see them at Dixons licking their lips as they approach the latest gizmo on display, nervously checking for observers and CCTV. The device shimmers at them, an intolerable tease after months of unconsummated hype. With the gadget finally in their sweaty paws, they bite their bottom lip and fondle its sleek black fascia, shuddering with ecstasy as they tentatively probe unprotected ports under the guise of checking for a USB socket. The gadget-lover's energy is soon spent and they reach below for a boxed item then head to the checkout. The display unit is left soiled with fingerprints and sweat, without so much as a fiver tucked into its metaphorical lacy panties. Two weeks later it's the same act all over again, with some other glossy doodah.

When these gadget fetishists aren't drooling over tiny electronics in real life, they go online to find out what the next pointless innovation will be. There's plenty of great gadget websites out there, but this one best captures how enthusiasts truly feel:

www.gadgetsexpose.com

As Gadgets Exposé it's pretty tame—a blog covering the latest stuff from Japan. But visit Gadget Sex Pose and you'll be left in no doubt about just how much some people love electronics.

CHAPTER FIVE

The Best of British

We Brits moan constantly. Miraculously, our offspring in America and Australia seldom express even a hint of cynicism, like toddlers who still believe in Father Christmas. While the yanks cheer "Yes we can!" we sigh in resignation and grumble "You can't do that, you'll put your back out."

The drongos on the other side of the world are just as irritating: tanned and cheerful, and frustratingly good at sporting pastimes we invented—most of the time.

The down-to-earth New World attitude produces big beastly Slurls, right there in front of you waving their metaphorical nob in your face. British Slurls are different because the British attitude is different: we would never call a website "I Love Big Al's!" or "Go Red Foxes!" We just don't like Big Al that much, and even if we did, we wouldn't declare it to the world. And the Red Foxes can stay right where they are, thank you very much—we won't we embarrassing ourselves with that.

When it comes to silly place names, we have ones that easily rival Cumming—such as Bell End, Muff, Happy Bottom, and the aforementioned Cocks. Slurls could easily occur with such great source material: for example, when creating a website for Muff's scuba club, or a forum for people who dislike the village of Cocks.* So far we have dodged such obvious disasters.

---

* Many hate websites are called something-sucks. So many, in fact, that companies often register their own "sucks" URLs to prevent disgruntled customers and ex-employees getting their hands on them. You know it's a perverse world when Google owns *googlesucks.com*.

Despite our natural reserve and cynicism Britain has proven to be a fertile breeding ground for Slurls. Mysteriously, they tend to fall in one of two diametrically opposed camps: pure filth or forgivably subtle.

Let's take a look at the Slurls of Britain, from the ridiculous to the sublime, and back to the ridiculous again. And oh, to any Americans reading this, there is no Santa Claus! Cackle.

Twitching Curtains

Mr Saunders is sitting in the plush head office of La Drape International Ltd, discussing the marketing strategy for his designer fabrics company with the management team.

"What we need is a website," *pronounces young Finbarr excitedly. Finbarr loves the web, and would like nothing more than to design a site for his father's business.*

"Interesting . . . " *replies Daddy Saunders, "*. . . what shall we call it?"

"On the Interweb you need a really short snappy name that people can remember," *says Finbarr, hinting at a knowledge he does not possess.* "How about ladrape.co.uk?"

"That's certainly short and snappy," *says Mr S,* "but won't it bring to mind forced buggery, like the stomach-curdling borstal glasshouse scene in the film Scum?"

"Ha ha, no of course not," *chortles Finbarr,* "no one would think that! It's all about curtains!"

Maybe it didn't happen quite like that, but the end result is the same:

www.ladrape.co.uk

The curious thing about La Drape—ignoring the website here—is it looks fine on paper but you only need to say it aloud to realise it's not quite right. Go on, say "We need some designer curtains, how about La Drape?" Careful now, say it in private, don't shout it across the pub.

Lad Rape, sorry, La Drape, have a sister site called The Quilted Wall where they advertise "bespoke fabric walling solutions to meet your wildest dreams." In other words, they glue blankets, duvets, and other bits of rag to the wall. That doesn't feature in any of my dreams, and definitely not the wildest ones.

Given their skill with names, I wonder what's next for this business. Perhaps they should start a new site selling leather drapes, called *beefcurtains.com*? Or they could flog ceremonial tapestries at *ritualhangings.com*. Both good ideas. You saw them here first.

Wind Power

Imagine the scene. It's a hot Saturday in July and Lorenzo heads out to the open-air pool. He wants to show off his lean physique, so pulls on a pair of tight swimming trunks. As he strides around the water, he senses the admiring eyes of reclining young ladies, and smiles to himself.

Then, disaster! An involuntary guff erupts, and the trunks inflate into a stinky zeppelin. The girls contort their faces in disgust. Lorenzo is mortified. That, dear reader, is known as:

www.speedofart.com

And the oddly-named website of a TV advertising art director, who has created a formula for the speed of art.*

---

* For the Maths geeks, it's "a function of life plus fiction, fiction tending to zero". In the unlikely scenario that you are intrigued by that, visit *www.speedofart.com/theory*.

Everything's For Sale

I admire the National Gamete Donation Trust. They've got balls. Their sperm-donation site *Give A Toss* (*giveatoss.com*) coaxes visitors with desktop wallpapers, spunky facts, and an adorable game called the Toss-O-Meter. The Meter is charged by moving the mouse in a wanking motion so rapid it would cause friction burns on a real member, while being egged on by a jaunty tune and girls in "I want your sperm" t-shirts. Move over, Grand Theft Auto IV.

That's the supply lines sorted out, but where can you go if you're in the market as a buyer? Well, there's always:

`www.cumstore.co.uk`

So roll up, roll up! Here at Cum Store we've got every type of sperm imaginable. What do you want your child to be? A basketball-playing brain surgeon, no problem! Heart-breakingly gorgeous with a PhD in genetic engineering? Piece of cake. Or if you're feeling adventurous you can get a lucky dip from our pick-and-mix range.

Sadly, *cumstore.co.uk* has been taken by a much more mundane business: Cumbria Storage Systems Ltd. They sell warehouse equipment like racking, sack trucks, and hot-melt glue guns (I don't think that's a euphemism).

Not content with a silly site name, Cumbria Storage Systems have based themselves in the town of Cockermouth. Perverts.

A Cock and Bull Story

Bullshit is the unlikely subject of much philosophical debate. In his essay *On Bullshit*, Harry Frankfurt of Princeton University says bullshit is a type of deceit, but different from lying. In *Deeper into Bullshit*, Gerald Cohen pooh-poohs Frankfurt, defining bullshit as nonsense presented as sense, produced either accidentally or deliberately. This is known in bullshit studies as the "Frankfurt vs. Cohen debate". I'm not making this up. Prudish students of bullshit call their subject "tauroscatology"—a little amusement in there for you Latin scholars.

Frankfurt and Cohen ignore the wider issues in bullshit studies, like "why are you wasting your time discussing crap?", and completely overlook the most obvious literal definition. In the developing world they really know what bullshit is, putting all forms of cow dung to good use. It is used as fertilizer, cooking fuel, insect repellent, steam engine sealant, insulation, and an ingredient in mud bricks. True stuff, once again. Some cultures also use it for an exfoliating spa treatment, handy shoes, and an amusing floppy hat. Probably.

Some occupations in the Western world also make good use of bullshit, at least in its figurative sense. These include salespeople of every sort, from estate agents to market traders, but also other people who talk for a living—teachers, for example.

These talented individuals have to keep their skills up to scratch, so this website makes complete sense:

`www.teachersbs.co.uk`

I don't know about you, but my teachers produced a lot of that. They also had a good line in waffle, produced excellent flannel, and always rounded off lessons with a bit of baloney.

But here's a strange thing: I couldn't find any advice about BS on the website, just a load of bumf about mortgages and savings. Oh, and something about The Teachers Building Society.

Fart For Art's Sake

One Off Art sells original paintings created in a studio near Tower Bridge, London. Works are available from stock or can be specially commissioned.

One of the painters featured on the site has a typical artistic temperament, describing their piece *Let Me Be* with "[*its*] deep rich colour gives off the I want to be alone signal." Their painting *Alone* is captioned "deep rich colour disguises the feelings." But the real tour-de-force is *Confused World*, explained with "GSCE's driving me mad, parents don't understand me, I don't understand me, aaaaaaaaaaaaarrrrghh." Take a few deep breaths, my unhinged friend.

www.oneoffart.co.uk

Re-imagining the site as "One of Fart" fits well. They even helpfully advise that you "open the windows" but scarily encourage you to "refresh your walls". Wouldn't that require a disastrous follow-through?

You might buy a painting from One Off Art, but would you buy perfume from www.scentofart.com*? This site offers services from web design to custom car paint jobs, and—oh yes—even sells art-inspired fragrances. They now use a sensibly hyphenated URL.*

Service Your Boiler

Northern Gas install heating systems all over England. They are based in Wolverhampton—which, incidentally, is in the Midlands, not the North. Try telling that to Southerners who think the North starts at Watford (which is in the South) and that the Midlands don't exist (which they do).

www.northerngasheating.com

Despite the geographical confusion, Northern Gas probably do good business in the North, which has a cooler climate than the South. And it's not just the weather that differs—there are many cultural and economic variations between the regions.

For example, a foreign visitor to this website might conclude that one popular Northern pastime is "gash eating".* After all, Northern Gas have helpfully posted a beginners guide, and they implore every visitor to regularly service their "boiler"—an affectionate Northern term for "wife". Cruelly, they suggest replacing boilers over ten years old as they don't perform nearly as well as younger models.

---

* I'll accept that the foreign visitor might have to come from Mars to reach that conclusion, but that still counts as foreign.

Hurt Me Plenty

Spain is a great holiday destination, but it's not without its risks: go to the wrong resort and you will suffer a Brits-on-the-piss rampage of tattooed yobs. And that's just the women. The men are the ones slavering at their heels, gently wooing them by waving their willies around and shouting "oy-oy!"

Young Brits abroad have a *terrible* reputation for heavy drinking and lewd behaviour. Well, terrible in the sense that they are looked upon badly for it, but actually a fantastic reputation in the sense of doing lots of it and taking it as far as possible.

The problem hasn't got past embarrassed British embassies, who have to spring offenders out of police cells and pay for stomach pumps. A Foreign Office campaign stresses the dangers of everything from accidents and sunburn to assault and STDs.* To headline their crusade they selected the eloquent phrase "Don't be a Dick". A better choice would have been "Choose Spain, Not Pain"—there's already a website for it:

www.choosespain.com

Unfortunately it's already in use, by a company called Choose Spain Ltd. They offer apartments, cottages and villas to rent in sunny España. For some reason I don't fancy going there now.

---

* That's sexually transmitted diseases, not subscriber trunk dialling. The latter has fallen out of use since they banned elephants from working in telephone exchanges.

CHAPTER SIX

The Naughty Corner

You may have noticed a reliable rule of thumb: the best Slurls are the crudest Slurls. Why is that? Well, sex has always sold, but the web is its new spiritual home. Products that in the past were traded only in shops with blacked-out windows are easily available on the net: aphrodisiacs, dildos, gimp suits, triple-headed petrol-engine butt plugs. You name it, you can get it, and lots more besides; items that require a bang up-to-date copy of *Gray's Anatomy* and a degree in perversion to put a name to. All this is available 24/7, in complete anonymity, delivered to your door.

The oldest and most successful kind of internet sex-business is pornography: it's a hundred billion dollar enterprise globally, a third of all websites are porn, and the annual spend in South Korea is over five hundred dollars per head. No wonder North Korea is separated by a huge fence—they don't want saucer-eyed Southies pouring over the border demanding golden showers and bukkake* from their hard-up neighbours. It's lucky the rest of the world is protected by sea.

Anyway, if you have a website that isn't sex-related, you don't want to be confused with sites that peddle porn or flog Viagra, do you? Pick a name that sounds filthy and people will leap to the conclusion that you are yet another pustule on the

---

* If you don't know what bukkake is, I haven't got the stomach to tell you. Just imagine the level of perversion you would need to get your rocks off if you spent $500 a year on internet porn.

grimy underbelly of the world wide ~~wank~~ web (oops). Didn't anyone tell this lot?

Hot Stuff

The Dickson Company of Addison, Illinois, has been making precision temperature, humidity, and pressure monitors since 1923.

www.dicksonweb.com

In the female-fixated world of porn, the idea of dicks-on-web should be refreshing: while men are gawping at gynaecological photos of ladies, women can satisfy their own desires with an endless slideshow of boners. Surely they would find that erotic? Actually, no. The problem, I am reliably informed, is that women do not find brightly-lit anatomical photography all that arousing.

Instead, your average woman is turned on by the prospect of a deep emotional relationship with an unrealistically caring, rich and subservient partner. With lofty ideals like that, your average man will always fall short. But some males are a bit special and, through the rosé-tinted wine goggles of picky ladies, offer a hint of perfection at first sight.

If there were dating websites for these special groups of men, the first place of interest might be called *almostgay.co.uk*. This would showcase straight men who enjoy shopping and romantic comedies, work out a lot and dance without inhibition. Certainly a woman's dream catch, but they're likely to run off with the plumber ten years down the line.

The second group are in their natural habitat online, and at *gratefulgeeks.com* could be captured in one of the databases they so adore. Computer boffins like online dating because it makes a frightening social activity resemble a computer game. Ladies are in the position of power here, providing the borderline autistic with an escape route to the real world. But geeks don't find reality all that appealing, preferring a raid on Lara Croft's virtual treasure box to a lady's real one.

A final (but perhaps desperate) place to look might be *uglybutpowerful.com*, featuring a range of female favourites including politicians, business men and aristocrats. Yellow teeth, eyes akimbo and flabby jowls are somehow made insignificant by an air of authority and a fat wallet. But these are womanisers par excellence, and their next conquest will be lined up quicker than you can say "personal assistant".

That all sounds a little hopeless for the ladies, but don't despair. What you need is a real man: a paunchy, farting, tactless oaf of a male. We may fester on the sofa drinking beer and scoffing nuts, but we'll probably stick around for the long run, and might even take the rubbish out if you ask nicely. Life would be much simpler, if only you could be content with dicks-on-web.

The Dickson Company had a change of heart in 2007 and moved their site to dicksondata.com. *Lucky data.*

Whatever Floats Your Boat

Upstate New York is mostly rural with a handful of small cities—a far cry from the vast metropolis of New York City. Many people outside the US (and some thickos inside) don't know that there is a state called New York. They only know of the Big Apple, Gotham, The Empire City: NYC.

Let me introduce one of the city's lesser-known websites:

```
www.nycanaltimes.com
```

So then, what to make of the NYC Anal Times? If I know the net, it must be an open-minded New Yorker's blog, covering their exploration of the region's less lovely sights. Or a porn-movie parody of the *New York Times*: a newspaper office drama where the shouting matches always result in improbable back-door action.

But it's time to face reality: The New York *Canal* Times is an online newspaper for people who use upstate New York's 524-mile canal system. It's just about buggering around on boats!

There's also a site called nycanal.com, *which is about—you guessed it—canals. Official government website* nyscanals.gov *managed to buck this particular naming trend.*

Get Rid of Dead Wood

Viagra has an interesting history. Created with the lofty aim of treating high blood pressure and angina, hospital trials went badly until a peculiar side effect was noticed. I've heard that on the final day of testing, when researchers had given up all hope, a nurse was taking an elderly subject's blood pressure and nearly lost an eye when he spontaneously produced a massive erection. He apologized profusely, astonished that a penile hibernation lasting twenty years had been broken, then promptly had a heart attack and died.

Well, that could be how it happened; I just made it up. For all I know, participants were wandering around with stiffies for days while petrified nurses carefully edged around the sides of the ward.

However its effects were discovered, pharmaceutical company Pfizer wasn't shy and advertised Viagra on American TV, complete with celebrity endorsements from Bob Dole* and Pelé—even though you needed a prescription to get it. Many of those who hankered for Viagra didn't relish a trip to the doctor, and the internet craze for "Vitamin V" was born. Soon millions of emails spewed forth advertising the pills, using subject lines like "V!@gra" to confuse dim-witted spam filters.

---

* Ancient American politician fond of referring to himself in the third person. The dirty talk of his revived love life—"Bob Dole wants it like this . . . Bob Dole's gonna lick that"—must be truly terrifying.

Given the stellar reputation of the drug as a quick-fix for a common problem, regulars at The Brewers Droop (in Bentley Wood, Wiltshire*) might hope to buy some from:

`www.viagrafix.com`

They would be disappointed, because that was the website of ViaGrafix Corporation—an Oklahoma company making training and design software, with a sideline as a local internet service provider.

They got their Slurl through misfortune, not incompetence, as they were formed in 1990, eight years before Viagra went on sale. The company was sold in 1999, at the height of the dotcom boom, and the unfortunate domain name disappeared into history—no doubt amidst much giggling, as the little blue pill had become a household name.

Dick's Lumber, the largest trade building supplies company in Western Canada, has a related website: dickslumber.com, sounding like a lumber yard with a distinct lack of wood. The moral of this story can—uniquely—be expressed with two Slurls: when you have Dick's Lumber you need ViaGrafix. Dot com.

---

* OK, you got me. It's a real pub and a real place, but you won't find one in the other. Nor will the pub's regulars, come to think of it.

Intimate Service Providers

Australian internet service provider (ISP) iiNet is in an unusual position: they have two Slurls. The first was picked up in 2003 with the acquisition of rival ISP WebOne, based in Perth.

www.webone.com.au

iiNet are still using the WebOne domain name. In the same year they also acquired New Zealand's third-largest ISP, a company called ihug, and have kept that URL going too:

www.ihug.com.au

So we bone, but I hug. iiNet has stayed in that spirit by calling their broadband-and-phone package "Naked DSL". Now, how do you want your Naked DSL? You can get it rough and ready from a group by visiting *webone.com.au* or warm, cuddly and on an individual basis at *ihug.com.au*. Either way, both group boning and personal hugging are naked (DSL). Take your pick.

Sixteen Inch Meat Feast

In most industries it's women who get the raw deal: menial jobs, low pay and poor opportunities. But there is one profession where men are the underdogs. In this industry male workers earn an average of $40,000 per year while women can easily notch up $100,000 to $250,000. Men are seldom recognised for their efforts, while females in equivalent roles get all the credit. In fact, the status of men is so low in this line of work that their bosses keep them almost completely out of the picture, while women bask in the limelight. Oh yes, male porn actors have it bad. Well, apart from the constant freaky sex with hundreds of beautiful women. Other than that it's a tough life.

But what happens to male porn stars when they get old? Well, they pack up their dumbbells, donate excess K-Y Jelly to the Salvation Army, and call up the beauty parlour to cancel their back, sack and crack subscription. Then they retire to a beautiful island paradise, just for male porn actors:

www.isleofmanmeat.com

Yes, an island all of their own. It's only fair after spending so much time at the bottom. Of the career ladder, of course. On the Isle of Man-Meat elderly cock-jockeys can sit back and relax in a place that's just like home: the plumbing never gets fixed, the radio stations play constant bow-chicka-wah-wah, and there's no such thing as an inappropriate erection.

Oh, all right. It's actually a site selling meat from the Isle of Man, run by a farmers' co-operative on the island. Their slogan: "You Can't Beat Our Meat". Well, not really. But it should be.

Naughty Tentacles

If I told you I had just been watching a cartoon, you would probably think I meant a piece of children's entertainment: maybe a heart-warming Disney movie with a solid moral compass. Or an amusing classic like Bugs Bunny or Scooby Doo. You probably wouldn't think I meant animated hardcore pornography.

It's a troubling combination, but animated porn does exist and it's popular stuff. It can trace its roots back to the 1930s and Betty Boop, who originally had a boyfriend/pet dog called Bimbo, and appeared in storylines where villains attempted to deflower her. The Hays Code of censorship came into effect in the same decade, outlawing Betty's dog-friend on the grounds of bestiality and covering her bare legs—like Hollywood's own private Taliban.

Fast-forward to today, and the bonkers Japanese have taken adult animation to extremes. Japan's animated porn movies are known as *hentai*, and cover every fetish you can possibly think of plus a few more, such as tentacle erotica. Naughty tentacles are not new though—they have been a staple of Japanese art for a long time, notably in the 1820 woodcut *The Dream of the Fisherman's Wife* by Katsushika Hokusai, which depicts a lady having sex with two octopi: a big one buried in the muff while a little one gives her a kiss. Quite sweet really.

Octopi are now old hat and the naughty tentacles are more likely to belong to aliens or monsters. Mid-1990s tentacle-rape epic *La Blue Girl* features sex-mad ninja rapist demons from another dimension, and was banned outright in Britain. Now you know what's out there, imagine what you would find at:

www.michaelspornanimation.com

Presumably, a sweaty-palmed bloke called Mike who will animate whatever perverse acts you can crank out of your dirty little mind. But no. Michael Sporn Animation, a New York company founded in 1980, is headed up by a celebrated animator with eighteen awards and an Oscar nomination under his belt. They create perfectly wholesome children's entertainment. With strong demand for filthy cartoons, maybe it's time for a change of direction—they already have the URL for it.

In Your Face

Weird new sexual practices are popping up all the time, and they find their way into the mainstream surprisingly quickly. For example, MILF* was a tiny sub-genre of porn until it was catapulted by *American Pie* to become the fourth most popular acronym in showbiz (just a guess, it could be third).

Language changes constantly to accommodate these new expressions, so it's important to check that your favourite term hasn't been hijacked before shouting it from the rooftops. Personally, I described my pleasant countryside vacations as "cottaging holidays" for years until someone asked if I meant a tour of public lavatories known for lewd behaviour. Oh, the shame.

Oil of Olay have done a similar thing with their website:

```
www.dailyfacials.com
```

Back in 2000 satirical website The Register warned Oil of Olay that stubby-fingered customers could omit the S from their URL and arrive at a very different site—one that also promotes facials, using all-natural secretions and a very explicit method of application. Some believe this approach can also "visibly reduce the appearance of fine lines and wrinkles", but that's just an old MILF's tale.

---

* Mother I'd like to, um, fool-around-with. That is, pornography featuring attractive older ladies.

Hot (and Steamy) Off the Press

Tri-Plex Business Products is a printer based in Denville, New Jersey.

www.triplexbusiness.com

In the real world Tri-Plex has a hyphen to help avoid mix-ups, at the expense of a meaningless name: "triplex" is a word but "plex" ain't. But like so many before them, they threw good sense out the window when it came to their website which, as "Triple-X Business", sounds like a porn industry trade association. It's not, because that's the sensibly-named AITA (Adult Industry Trade Association)—in the UK, anyway. The US equivalent is called The Free Speech Coalition, bringing together great American talents for lobbying and euphemism.*

It's the job of trade associations to campaign on behalf of their industry, and The Free Speech Coalition is fighting against a proposed new top-level domain name (TLD) of ".xxx"—literally triple-x. Dot-triple-x would provide porn producers with an alternative to dot-com domains, but the Free Speech Coalition doesn't like it, fearing a mandatory dot-triple-x porn-ghetto.

Applicants for dot-triple-x domain names, if they ever become a reality, would have to pass special eligibility rules.

---

* They are beaten for sheer balls-out cheek by the Air Quality Standards Coalition (now defunct), who lobbied *against* air quality regulations on behalf of oil, haulage and car companies.

Whereas most terms and conditions on the internet prohibit obscene or offensive material, dot-triple-x would positively require it, conjuring up the surreal scenario of a registration being rejected because their proposed content just isn't filthy enough. Group sex—that's fine, but just boobies? No way! What are you, some kind of morally upstanding pervert?

CHAPTER SEVEN

The World Laughs With You

T he UK and US have the lion's share of Slurls, but the rest of the world likes to get in on the act too. Crazy as it sounds, not everybody in the world speaks English as a first language, and some don't speak it at all!

To be fair to these Johnny Foreigners, I will overlook websites that are not aimed at speakers of our global lingua franca.* That's a pardon for *feeduscrap.com* (French), *campanal.com* (Spanish), *www.anker.com* (German) and *apetit.com* (Finnish but with a penchant for French—go figure). Quelle domage, I liked the idea of a site about monkey mammaries.

Happily, lots of our friends abroad like to dabble in the Queen's lingo. It's a wonderful thing when far flung people innocently create misnomers of staggering proportions. And completely mind-boggling when they (in theory) speak English as a first language.

You'll soon discover that international Slurls are a strange breed, the flightless birds of this universe. Squawking and eyeing us with curiosity, they waddle straight into danger. So let's take our Slurls tour global, starting with a country that has made a beautiful, beautiful contribution to this field. The Cook Islands, we salute you.

---

* Which, perversely, means "Germanic language"—so a backdoor victory for the schnitzel munchers.

Dot Cock

It's a rare and happy occasion when an entire country gets in on the Slurls act. That country is the Cook Islands: a state of fifteen small volcanic islands in the South Pacific, associated with New Zealand.

Now, bear with me while I give you a little background on how dot cock came to be. The Internet Assigned Numbers Authority is responsible for doling out country domains and dutifully gave the Cook Islands ".ck", following the international ISO standard. Some countries decide to use a second level of codes, which indicate the kind of organisation the website belongs to. For example, in the UK we have *.co.uk* for companies, *.ac.uk* for academic institutions, *.gov.uk* for government agencies, and so on. The UK has a population of sixty million and we enjoy bureaucracy, so the second-level system works well for us.

The Cook Islands has a population of just under twenty thousand, but they decided they also needed second-level categories to differentiate between their undoubtedly vast number of organisations. They chose:

- ❖ **.edu.ck**: educational institutions
- ❖ **.gov.ck**: government agencies
- ❖ **.co.ck**: business organisations

Clearly, someone was having a laugh. Sadly that sense of humour ran out at some point (probably after the thousandth request to register *suckmy.co.ck*), and now the Cook Islands doesn't allow any old dot cock to be registered. Obscene domains like *huge.co.ck* are rejected and future requests for the same name ignored. A less bashful country would have made a fortune from pornographers and perverts, and welcomed droves of tourists to the dot cock museum.

Nevertheless, it's easy to enjoy almost any domain that ends dot cock. Here are my personal favourites:

`www.google.co.ck`

The Cook Islands version of the world's most popular website. Could also be an insult, meaning "your penis is so small you need a search engine to find it."

`www.palm.co.ck`

A Cook Islands Dive Shop. Another potential insult, meaning "one who can't keep his giggle stick out of his hands."

`www.budget.co.ck`

The Cook Islands branch of car rental company Budget. They could do a good sideline in cut-price gigolos—unwashed and hairy, but great value for money. That's a clever business angle, because in tough economic times, who's going to splash out on full-priced cock?

`www.travel.co.ck`

A Cook Islands travel agent. Also a pocket-sized dildo you can take on trips with you. Maybe.

Kudos to Charlie Brooker and Chris Morris, writers of sitcom Nathan Barley, in which the title character registers his website in the Cook Islands, and refers to it as "trashbat dot cock".

Face The Music

MP3's Hits is a searchable database of free music downloads. As the internet's 26,405th most visited website, it is the most popular Slurl in the world.

www.mp3shits.com

MP3's Hits (of course) is something of a case study in globalisation. A Russian-owned website, in English, which attracts more visitors from Japan than any other country. After Japan, its visitors come from India, the United States, South Africa, and Pakistan.

MP3's Hits promises the latest albums for free, which sounds appealing, but also a little on the naughty side. If you've seen the anti-piracy adverts you will know that downloading music without paying guarantees a place in hell, in a bit several degrees hotter than the section for child murderers and holocaust deniers. How it rates so much worse than yesteryear's low-tech efforts of recording tunes off the radio or making a mix tape is a bit of a mystery.*

Even if you can avoid eternal damnation, downloading stuff that you normally have to pay for is fraught with danger—

---

* Just to be clear: I have never recorded anything off anything, and only once watched a pirated film but I didn't know it was a rip-off and my eyes didn't inhale.

cyber criminals have no softer target than people who want something for nothing (although gullibility is a welcome bonus).

Despite the name, MP3's Hits is at the respectable end of freebie sites. If you visit the seedier establishments, expect at least a bevy of pop-up windows advertising casinos and weight-loss pills. That's not so bad, and may even evoke a wave of nostalgia for 1990s-style web surfing. But if you visit these sites and find a path through the pop-ups to the promised free download, there's a chance that nothing will happen when you run it on your computer.

Or so it appears. For all you know your computer will be terminally infested with viruses and spyware. A Russian named Dmitry will assume your identity, sell your children into slavery, turn your house into a brothel, and slap you senseless with a genuine CD of the track you tried to get for free. Piracy is not a victimless crime, you know.

Before mobile phones could play standard MP3s, people who liked to inflict their poor taste in music on the general public would buy specially created ringtones, hang around at bus stops, and pretend to receive calls. One ringtone vendor shared MP3's Hits talent for naming: ringtoneshits.com. *They disappeared in late 2007.*

Heidi Haters

Swissbit is a European manufacturer of high-quality computer memory chips. As a proud Swiss company, Swissbit has chosen to register their website in their home country.

`www.swissbit.ch*`

I know that computer technology is a male-dominated industry, but declaring institutional misogyny in your URL is taking it too far.

What have they got against Swiss women anyway? Surely they like Ursula Andress, best known for rising sexily from the sea as Bond girl Honey Ryder. She gave Jimmy Bond a tough time at first but ended up shagging him, so she's only a little bitchy. Maybe they don't like Swiss tennis player Martina Hingis, who's fond of slagging off opponents and received a two-year ban for cocaine use. I must admit that's *quite* bitchy.

Or could it be beloved little Swiss girl Heidi they can't stand? Well, I believe so. You see, just an hour down the road from Swissbit's HQ is one of the main tourist areas in Switzerland: Heidiland, an alpine paradise named after "the most famous girl in the world". Every year Heidiland is swamped by elderly Japanese tourists, who jump off the train, get snapped

---

* Switzerland's official (Latin) name is "Confoederatio Helvetica", hence the two-letter abbreviation "CH".

with St Bernard's wearing little barrels, then dash to the next photo opportunity squealing excitedly about Heidi, mountains, and edelweiss.

So Swissbit's geeks spend all day straining their brain cells over the latest thousand-gigabyte memory chips, but down in Heidiland all the Japanese tourists care about is stupid bloody Heidi prancing about the alpine meadows going "La la la, aren't I adorable?" Bloody Swiss bitch.

Play Station

Mole Station is a little place near the town of Tenterfield, in New South Wales, Australia. Mole Station Native Nursery grows shrubs, flowers and trees—mostly for wholesale.

www.molestationnursery.com

Judging from the name, it's not child-friendly—not from the child's point of view anyway; local nonces may think it's a great place for kids. Another local attraction is Mole Station Farmstay. So while youngsters are "looked after" at the nursery, older kids can get a taste of rural traditions at the farm. They do things differently out in the country.

Mole Station Native Nursery has upped sticks and moved to molerivernursery.com, *even though that isn't their name. Damn cheats.*

Selling Houses: The Oldest Profession?

Who are *The Professionals*? Are they Bodie and Doyle, lead characters of a 1970s TV series featuring lots of violence, sexism, dangerous driving and unnecessary rolls across the bonnet of a Ford Capri? Well, yes, but that was a long time ago. Now The Professionals are a New Zealand chain of estate agents—they aren't quite as exciting as Bodie and Doyle. For four years you could find these Professionals at:

```
www.professional-ho.co.nz
```

I have no quarrel with the professional part, but where did the ho come from? I've narrowed it down to three possibilities:

a. "Ho" is an unusual Kiwi abbreviation for "houses"

b. The Professionals' local offices have their own websites with different URLs, so this was the website for Head Office

c. Their programmer's favourite chemical element is Holmium (Ho) a highly magnetic substance used in nuclear control rods

Your guess is as good as mine.

The Professionals are now based at www.professionals.co.nz. *That's the estate agents, not the crime-fighting duo.*

Norwegian Wouldn't

For the sun-obsessed British, a holiday in Norway is a bizarre proposition. Where are the deckchair-crammed beaches? How much is a jug of sangria? Can you even *buy* an inflatable plastic ring in the shape of a seahorse there? Valid concerns, you might think. But despite its chilly climate, Norway has a lot to offer: fjords and lakes, woodlands and waterfalls, pure mountain air and a range of wholesome outdoor activities.

A good place to stay and experience all these wonderful sights is the Osnes Hyttepark (Osnes cabin park) located in Etne, on the South West coast of Norway. According to the official Norwegian tourism website, cabins in the Osnes Hyttepark have nice views, nice walks, nice boating facilities and a nice fish-gutting area. The park's multilingual website echoes that combination of a day immersed in beautiful scenery followed by a nasty slip on fish innards:

www.oh.no

Oh yes, combine the abbreviations for Osnes Hyttepark (OH) and Norway (NO) to evoke alarm, concern and resentment—hardly the hallmarks of a great vacation.

Glastonbury's Starting to Look Tame

Holland's Hit Festival is an annual music festival in Groningen, The Netherlands.

www.hollandshitfestival.nl

We all associate Holland with clogs, windmills and tulips, but modern Dutch clichés also include marijuana and extreme pornography. The Holland Shit Festival doesn't require a huge leap of imagination. Then again, it could just be a really awful festival.

In 2009 the site was the unlikely victim of a hacking attack, which replaced every page with a message protesting the treatment of the Uyghur ethnic group by the Chinese government. A clever move. Like most people, Chinese president Hu Jintao is surely a big fan of minor Dutch music festivals, so hacking Holland's Hit Festival will have made him think twice about oppressing minorities.

The rules have been bent with this one, because the site is in Dutch. On the other hand, most people in the Netherlands speak English very well, so they should have known better. The same goes for equally potty-obsessed website www.pisartfestival.nl *which, incidentally, is also a music festival—not an exhibition of yellow-streaked canvasses.*

Electric Ballroom

Contrary to internet folklore, this website has nothing to do with UK electricity generation company Powergen:

www.powergenitalia.com

It was actually registered in 2000 by an Italian company, also called Powergen, who make industrial battery chargers. It looks like they were keen to sell their products to English speakers so registered a dot-com domain name that wouldn't scare them away. It didn't work out. Potential customers were probably frightened by the prospect of plugging their testicles into the mains, and the site was abandoned.

You could argue that because the English word for Italy is, well, *Italy*, the site should have been called powergenitaly.com—which is an L away from being equally as good. Given the choice, would you rather power genitalia or power genitally? How would you go about doing either?

Recently Powergen (the Italian one) launched a new "special" product, called the Chopper Charger. They're up to their old tricks again.

The Power Genitalia site is no longer active, but you can still see it as it was using the Internet Archive—the web's equivalent of a shop selling photos from the 1950s.

Curl Up With the Good Book

CUM Books is a South African chain of Christian bookshops. Its name is derived from the initials of parent company Christelike Uitgewers Maatskappy—Afrikaans for "Christian Art Publishers".

www.cumbooks.co.za

I think that gives false hope. Imagine a sex-starved Afrikaner, eyes boggling and balls bulging, wandering around his local shopping mall and stumbling into a branch of CUM Books. He enters with hope in his heart, thinking "dat is wat Ek soek"* but is confronted with books on spiritual growth, Christian living, and advanced prayer techniques. Desperate times call for desperate measures, but you can't sink much lower than trying to bang one out over the Bible.

Then again, perhaps not all is lost, because there *are* some saucy minxes in the Good Book. That may come as a surprise, because the Bible is not generally known for stories about hotties. But actually there are plenty of Biblical bimbos—enough to populate a surreal online survey called "Which Biblical Slut

---

* Literally "That is what I seek" in the beautiful Afrikaans language. Well, they think it's beautiful. I think it sounds like a drunk five-year old speaking English in a comically low voice, and randomly changing every other vowel.

Are You?"* This little gem includes ever-so-slightly leading questions like:

What do you do when you see a man you like?
  a) *Beg for forgiveness.*
  b) *Betray my city to help him.*
  c) *Sleep with him. I'm a prostitute; it's what I do.*
  d) *. . .*

Answer all eight questions to discover if you are Delilah (strength-stealing slut), Gomer (symbolic slut), one of Solomon's 300 concubines (sluts, the bloody lot of 'em), Potiphar's Wife (spurned slut), The Woman Who Was Not Stoned (nameless slut), Tamar (baby-obsessed slut), or Rahab (reformed royal slut). Basically, it's the Bible re-imagined as a succession of stories about sluts. The good people at CUM Books would not approve.

---

* You can get to it via *tinyurl.com/biblical-sluts*

Jail Birds In the Trees

Les Bocages (meaning "the groves") is a tree surgery business based in Brittany, France. Its website is mostly in English, reflecting its target customers: the region's British immigrants and second-home owners.

www.lesbocages.com

Website visitors expecting information on *Prisoner: Cell Block H* will be disappointed: the cult TV drama about a women's jail, which featured more than a little lady-love, is completely overlooked. The series ran for nearly seven hundred episodes, and was simply called *Prisoner* in its native Australia. It couldn't be screened with that name in the UK, due to the similarity with bonkers spy drama *The Prisoner.** With hindsight, they should have called it *Lesbo Cages*—a much snappier name, and just as accurate.

---

* You know, the one with Patrick McGoohan and the inexplicably menacing big white balloon.

CHAPTER EIGHT

Trading Insults

W hen someone visits us at home or work we do our best to make them feel welcome. Since childhood we have been taught to put people at their ease with a simple greeting, a chat about the weather, or the offer of a drink. The common courtesies that make this harsh world a nicer place to be; easy, painless, and the start of every civil conversation.

If someone visits your website, do the same rules apply? Of course they do! Web designers work hard to make their sites attractive, compelling, and easy to use. When someone comes to your website—a global window on your business—you *could* greet them by saying:

- ❖ You stink!
- ❖ Bend over!
- ❖ Fuck off!
- ❖ I've watched you on the lavatory!

Would *you* say that to a guest? Of course you wouldn't, but it's what the businesses in this chapter appear to do. We can only hope it doesn't cross over into the real world like a epidemic of unusually inventive Tourette's. If it did, a trip to Currys to buy a toaster would be greeted with "My arse in your face!" Visit Starbucks for a mocha-chocca-chino and they'd hand over the drink not with a thank-you but with "I shit in the milk".

Actually, that's a genuine Spanish curse. Bizarrely, it means "damn my bad luck"—so it's a jolly everyday phrase for toe-stubbings and minor spillages. A variant is "suck the butter from my ass". The general theme seems to be dairy products and poo, or maybe they're just fans of *Last Tango in Paris*.*

Still, the Spaniards can't compete with Arabian abuse. Their swearing fetishes include feet ("a shoe is on your head") and penises ("a thousand dicks in your religion"). I admire the imagination of international expletives, but we'll stick to English epithets here.

---

* In which Marlon Brando uses a good dollop of butter to help entertain a lady via the, um, tradesman's entrance. Movie magazine Premiere ran a poll in 2007 to discover the greatest ever cinematic lines and *Last Tango's* "Go, get the butter" was voted as number 67. Brando appears again at number 66 with *Apocalypse Now's* "The horror . . . the horror . . ." Coincidence?

Och Aye, It's a Wee Camera

You'll have to forgive me a bit of text-speak with this one, but it's worth it—I promise. This next site rounds up funny videos on the internet, promising good clean family fun and safe-for-work humour. Strange then, that it can be found at:

www.icup.tv

If iCup.tv had hidden-camera videos of folk, well, peeing, that might not be very pleasant but would fit the name perfectly—I see you pee TV.

It could also be very profitable for them, because some people like to watch while others take a Jimmy Riddle—that kind of thing turns them on.

Finding urination erotic is a fetish known as urophilia, or golden showers. To be honest, if you didn't know what it was, wouldn't a golden shower sound wonderful? It evokes a warm spray from above, tinted with an amber glow, like washing in tropical rain as the sun sets over the Amazon. Someone who works in advertising, with an urge to promote his unusual hobby, must have coined that one.

Urophiles sometimes hit the news after hiding cameras in lavatories. It's hard to imagine being so driven to watch women peeing that you would install a camera, but it happens. In one case a Scottish lawyer put a camcorder in a toilet *next to his office*, hidden in a cardboard box—hardly a regular piece of toilet furniture. After a week a secretary noticed the box and, peeking inside, probably exclaimed "Och aye, it's a wee camera!"

Now urophilia has come out of the cubicle and found its way into urinals moulded into the shape of ladies' lips. Lips that are wide-open, pouting, and wearing bright red lipstick. They're called *Kisses!*, and are made by Bathroom Mania of the Netherlands. Yes, kisses. Big, open-mouthed, urine-gargling smackers. Lovely. These designer piss-pots have found their way into a Dutch branch of McDonalds, and were planned for the Virgin Airways Clubhouse in New York's John F Kennedy airport. They were removed from the McDonalds and abandoned by Virgin, following complaints. Urophiles everywhere cancelled their flights.

BioScan Screening Systems of Tennessee make a urine specimen container called the iCup, which includes a drug-testing kit. Urine tests can be cheated with a sneaky bag of clean wee, so the tester really does want to see you pee. Unlike iCup.tv, BioScan's iCup is a great bit of naming.

Go Relocate Yourself

Effective Office Environments, based in Cincinnati, Ohio, supply office furniture and provide relocation management services.

`www.effoff.com`

Nice. But could there be a twisted logic at play? Relocations are stressful events—people get upset. When you break the news of a move there's plenty of well-wishing and good-lucking in public, but those left behind are often bitter, thinking "Go on then, eff off."

In that vein, this could be a great ad campaign for Effective Office Environments:

Need to move office in a hurry? All those boxes and files getting you down? Help is at hand from Effective Office Environments, or Eff Off for short. We have ten years' experience in skedaddling, unmatched skill in vamoosing, and lead the industry in get the hell away from me!

Eff Off—We'll Tell You Where To Go!

So *that's* what relocation management services are.

This isn't cheating, eff is a real word, at least in my dictionary. And yes, it's a proper big one, not Roger Mellie's Profanisaurus.

OMG WTF LOL

Internet slang is a new vocabulary used in online forums, chat rooms and instant messaging to save typing and express emotion. In just a few years it has become incredibly popular. The most common term is LOL, which represents laughter—it stands for "laughing out loud". Other frequently used acronyms are OMG—oh my God—and WTF, an exclamation of surprise meaning "what the flip?" (or something very similar).

These acronyms are instantly recognisable to experienced web users, but completely perplexing to newcomers, creating a language gap that's difficult to bridge. So much confusion is being spread that white-collar workers have to be warned not to use internet slang in their business communications. In my own experience of office work, OMG and WTF would have come in quite handy, but there was little call for LOL.

Internet slang has even crossed over into face-to-face conversation, and is used by teenagers in an endearingly postmodern and ironic way.* For example, roffle (a spoken version of ROFL—rolling on the floor laughing) is said aloud not to convey laughter but to say "I acknowledge your attempt at humour but I did not find it at all amusing on this particular occasion". To be fair, it wouldn't make a lot of sense to convey genuine laughter with "roffle"—it's probably best expressed by,

---

* I'm being post-modern and ironic here, because being post-modern and ironic isn't endearing at all. It's just annoying.

well, laughing. If you are under twenty you might not know what that last word means—it's the same as LOL-ing.

Anyway, I'll get to the point. Given the ubiquity of internet slang, it's probably not a great idea to give your organisation a name identical to a popular term. And if you had the name before the rise of geek-speak, you might want to think about changing it—or at least expanding it a little in the URL. Here's what happens if you don't:

`www.omfg.com`

OMFG is very similar in meaning to OMG, but stronger. And Official Meeting Facilities Guide is (they say) the leading meeting planning directory for meeting professionals. Now really, WTF?

`www.wtf.org`

The World Taekwondo Federation. Probably best not to laugh at champion martial artists . . . oh sod it, LOL!

`www.lol.org`

Website of the "Lord of Life" church in Ramsey, Minnesota. Presumably they kneel down every Sunday, bow their heads and begin "OMG who art in heaven . . ."

I Don't Know How to Break This to You

UST Inc. manufactures a range of chewing tobaccos and premium wines. They're based in Stamford, Connecticut, and, ahem—sorry but someone has to say it:

www.ustinc.com

I'm glad that's out in the open. Maybe you just need to wash more often? Do you use soap? A bit of deodorant wouldn't go amiss. As for your breath . . . OK, OK, I'm sorry. You don't smell, but that's more than I can say for anyone overusing UST's products: after a night glugging wine and eating tobacco they'll pong to high heaven. And a visit to UST's site will remind them of that.

To be completely accurate, UST make dipping tobacco, or "dip", rather than chewing tobacco. It still goes in your mouth, but you just hold it there rather than chomping on the stuff. Like when the flavour goes from chewing gum, but instead of spitting it out you get a strange satisfaction from moulding it into the space behind your upper lip. I'm not really seeing the attraction of doing that with a half-dried addictive plant.

Anyway, the modern industry term for dip is "moist smoke-less tobacco", which makes it sound not only harmless but positively delicious, and a little erotic. Smokeless, like a fresh spring day out in the mountains. Moist, like a teenage girl's crotch at a Busted concert. What could be more pure and wholesome? Smoking is on the decline, but stuffing tobacco in your mouth or snorting it up your nose is a growing market— never mind that it's completely gross and might cause cancer— it's only moist smokeless tobacco!

To the pedants out there: ustinc.com *may bend the rules by lapsing into text-speak but it seemed too good to pass up. I made the rules so I can break them—isn't that how the world works?*

Working Off the Debt

Benjamin Dover is a broadcaster, author and columnist on the topic of consumer rights and personal finance. He is, in his own words, "on a mission to raise America's Common Sense IQ."

`www.bendover.com`

As an ambassador for common sense, a man who can help when the banks have you over a barrel, it's strange that Ben fell for the oldest funny-name joke in the book. He's clearly aware that his moniker may raise a giggle because, when the surname is included, he always uses "Benjamin" on the site. But he's not a stickler for formality: it's "Ben" every time when he goes for a first-names-only basis. A sensible policy. He doesn't make any jokes about it either, and that's fair enough—he must have heard them all.

So why ignore all that and set out your stall at *bendover.com*? It's a mystery. The domain was registered in 1995 and in use the next year. In a moment of clarity in 1999 he registered *benjamindover.com*, but didn't completely change over to the name and now it's disappeared. But there's worse: British pornographer Steve Perry hit the big time in the mid-nineties with his *Ben Dover* series of gonzo pornographic movies.* Perry snapped up *ben-dover.com* and now you'll never find America's ambassador for common sense by searching for "Ben Dover"; only porn, filth, and more porn.

Benjamin Dover tried hard to avoid the obvious but fell at the last hurdle (or was it the first?) He could have followed the lead of North Carolina estate agent Michael Hunt, or Air Force Historian Dr William Head—neither fell into the trap with their self-named sites—but somehow that wasn't to be for our Ben.

Still, it's not too late for a change of tack. In his field the joke would run and run: we regularly get shafted with credit card debt, stiffed by loan sharks, and royally screwed over mortgage repayments. The only problem? With that name he should be batting for the other team (the banks, that is).

---

* Porn made in an amateur style where the cameraman takes part in the "acting". Seymore Butts is another top producer. Seriously.

CHAPTER NINE

Kids These Days

Ah, children. It's hard to know whether to love 'em or hate 'em. I blame television for this confusion. Primetime Saturday TV mainly consists of children at weddings trying to kiss each other and falling over. Adorable. But flick on the box at the same time on Monday and it's full of children boozing on street corners and stabbing passers-by. Are these truly the same creatures, now a few years older, that brought us to tears of laughter? What went wrong?

Well, it's all part of growing up. Kids change dramatically as they grow older, regressing into a feral state like frogs changing back into tadpoles. Instead of clambering into ponds, these tadpole-children form marauding gangs, hang around outside chip shops, and drink a sweet alcoholic liquid that has been coloured blue for no good reason. Therein lies a clue to their downfall: children just can't get enough of sugar. In fact, the average child's sugar dependency makes Amy Winehouse look like a nun. Well, a heavily tattooed nun, with a preposterous haircut.

Now where have we seen sugary blue things before? That's right: blue Smarties. These chocolaty discs of doom were introduced in 1989, a few short years before children went insane.* Is the introduction of blue Smarties and the rise of feral children a

---

* Right-wing writer Peter Hitchens was the first to write about "feral children", in 1997, but who's counting? He went on to call them a "generation of murderous, morally blank wolf-children". You can't make this stuff up.

coincidence? Maybe not. Blue Smarties contained the artificial colour E133, code-named Brilliant Blue. But, according to campaigners, they were far from brilliant: the cocktail of artificial colours found in a tube of Smarties could change a placid child into a simmering lunatic, they said.

In recent times the Smarties tube itself was changed in design from round to hexagonal—the shape of Satan's penis. Or so you might think, from the reaction of yet more campaigners with nothing better to get annoyed about. It would be understandable if you jumped to the conclusion that world hunger has been eradicated, and war abolished, now that so many people are getting upset about confectionary. Nestlé removed the artificial colours in 2006, resulting in soothing pastel-shaded Smarties, so we should soon see a new generation of youngsters coming through with markedly less psychosis.

So there you have it, the tabloid view of our precious little babies. If you subscribe to this view, you should enjoy the malice carried out on, by, and for children in this chapter. If you don't, read it anyway. Maybe you'll change your mind.

Bring Your Daughter . . . to the Slaughter

The Children's Laughter Foundation, based in Dallas, Texas, supports charities that fight abuse and neglect, improve children's medical treatment, and advance their educational and emotional development.

www.childrenslaughter.com

I'm a great believer in the power of laughter. It has a profound effect on the brain, activating the prefrontal cortex and releasing pleasure-giving endorphins—the body's equivalent to morphine. I'm not so convinced by the power of slaughter. But you can't spell slaughter without laughter, so maybe there's a connection.

The biological benefits of mirth are so profound they have inspired a new way of keeping fit called laughter yoga, which features breathing exercises, stretching, clapping, and creepy forced chanting of ho ho ha ha he he. Apparently it reduces stress and fights diabetes, high blood pressure, arthritis and cancer. According to Wikipedia there are now over 500,000 laughter yoga clubs in 400 countries—which is a fantastic achievement, especially when you consider that there are only 195 countries in the world. There are no statistics available on the number of slaughter yoga clubs.

Anyway, The Children's Laughter Foundation is all about the kids, healing the scars of their disadvantaged backgrounds and allowing them to play and laugh as children should. The sound of a child's laughter is an uplifting noise, so they say, like tiny bells ringing in heaven or angels sweetly singing. But that's not always the case. My best friend when I was eight years old was easily amused—he was reliably brought to tears by the word "piss". And his laughter was like a evil genius riding a donkey through a creaky door, normally accompanied by a large snot bubble under his left nostril. Heavenly!

. . . Every Class You Teach, I'll Be Watching You

Teaching is a worthwhile profession; a calling which brings knowledge and inspiration to children from across the social spectrum—without regard to race, colour, creed, or standards of personal hygiene.

TeachersTalk is a free resource for UK teachers. The highlight of the site is a forum for giving support and sharing advice.

www.teacherstalk.co.uk

Teachers know that each child has a different potential, and a few will be our doctors and lawyers while others will become serial killers. Most won't bask in such glories. But the average kid *will* collect a shed load of hang-ups from their schooldays: regrets, grudges, rejections and (for some) psychotic tendencies. Perhaps these are the people *teacherstalk.co.uk* should target? TeacherStalk: where twisted individuals with school fixations can track down, harass, and generally creep out teachers past and present.

So come on you weirdoes! Did Mr Jones say something slightly critical to you in a Maths lesson ten years ago? Has that comment been festering in your tiny little cesspool of a mind ever since? Wouldn't it feel good to daub graffiti on his car, send turds to his wife, and bully his children as they walk home from school? Of course it would!

At TeacherStalk you can get support and advice from other nut jobs, and the latest stalking news and reviews, all for one great value monthly subscription. When you receive your first restraining order, we'll even feature you in our "admit that you love me or I'll crap through your letterbox (again)" hall of fame. Join us now!

Shaven Havens

A Child's Haven was a day care centre and kindergarten based in the town of O'Fallon, Missouri.

www.achildshaven.com

This website is in the same vein as Molestation Nursery, but even more of an achievement: the Mole Station people grow plants but these folk from Missouri really do look after kids.

A childcare business called A Child Shaven is certainly a cause for concern, partly because it's a pointless practice: pre-pubescent children are essentially hairless, so shaving them gains you nothing. A notable exception is premature babies, and sometimes full-term newborns, who can be covered in a fine fur called lanugo. If this happens it's probably fine to give your furry little monkey baby a quick shave.

A Child's Haven is now called Little Guppy Child Development Center—a strange name, but not as strange as shaving children. The old domain name is parked, meaning it's full of automatically generated ads for credit cards and house insurance. The homepage includes a generic tagline, which paints a worrying picture, because it reads "Achildshaven.com: What you need, when you need it." To be honest, I could probably make do without one.

Sugar Biscuit Mother Trucker

Childrenswear.co.uk is an online clothing store specialising in formal wear for kids.

www.childrenswear.co.uk

Well, that's a fact of life. Children *do* swear, and when it happens it can be shocking, upsetting, or just plain funny. Kids must learn that bad language from somewhere. The main culprits are the playground, foul-mouthed adults, and television—a medium which is not only responsible for rises in violent crime and sexually transmitted diseases, but also widespread idiocy and the downfall of civilisation as we know it.

Most of the swearing on telly comes from two sources: celebrity chefs and members of the Osbourne family. Culinary cussing is not unwarranted, because swearing at food actually makes it taste better. No-one would earn a Michelin star without first telling their grouse pie to go fuck itself. The Osbourne children, poor little mites, may have inherited a rare genetic disorder from their father which would cause their brains to haemorrhage if they don't swear at least twice a minute. Even if Sharon doesn't have the condition, she joins in to keep them company.

There are all sorts of methods to deal with childhood swearing. Some will suggest amusing alternatives like "sugar biscuits" and "mother trucker". Others take a rational approach, explaining what the words mean and that they can hurt feelings.

And a few, missing the metaphor entirely, wash their little one's mouth out with soap and water. A troubling precedent. Would they follow up a warning that "the bogeyman will get you" with a midnight kidnapping and dismemberment in the woods? Probably. If you don't follow up on your threats they'll never respect you.

Now Spit!

The Boston Society for Dental Improvement promotes dentistry and dental health in the city of Boston, Massachusetts.

www.pedo.org

Yes, their website is called pedo, but let me explain before you go and beat up the nearest dentist, dental nurse, or (failing that) someone who has been to the dentist recently.* You see, Pedo is an abbreviation of Pedodontics, a branch of dentistry dealing with children. So breath a sigh of relief—they only want the kiddies of Boston to have healthy teeth and gums! Admittedly that's my own deduction, not an explanation I found on the site, but I hope and pray that it's the right one.

Anyway, a single website accidentally called pedo is one thing. Who would have thought there's another three? What's more, each arrived at the name by a different route:

www.apedo.com

The African Private Enterprise Development Organization, based in Corvallis, Oregon. One thing they do is build toilets in

---

* Paedophile hysteria hit a peak in 2000 when Welsh vigilantes attacked the home of an innocent paediatrician—a doctor specialising in child medicine. Not only did the mob get their words mangled, but they apparently thought paedophiles advertise the fact in their job title.

Africa. Personally, I'm a little too squeamish to use a toilet built by APEDO.

`www.ipedo.com`

Ipedo is a Silicon Valley company that makes database software. They give no clue to how their name arose, but isn't everything better when it starts with an I? Phones, books and pods are all much improved—maybe pedos too?

`www.carolinapedo.com`

This is a website for two paediatric dentistry practices in North Carolina; one in Wakefield and the other in Heritage. Each clinic boasts murals, toys, playhouses and more—just to reassure the kids. But a few toys are surely a poor consolation for a filling from the Carolina Pedo.

It just goes to show there's more than one way to skin a cat and, by the same token, more than one way to call your website pedo.

CHAPTER TEN

Faking It

They say the internet has brought the world together—a global village where everybody knows everybody, and a Peruvian cattle farmer will drop in for virtual coffee just as readily as Aunt Ethel will for a real one. In truth, the internet has chopped the world up into a million tiny cliques and cults; the Peruvian farmer may share a love of stained glass lampshades but we can no longer relate to the people next door. They're too busy chatting online about the bonus characters in Super Gimlet Dance Party with a Filipino ladyboy and a Norwegian police chief.

Each internet micro-cult comes with its own etiquette, customs, and language. The ultimate aim of online culture seems to be the development of a zillion hateful clans, each having their own indecipherable conversations and sneering at passers by who make the humiliating faux pas of confusing ROFL and RTFM.*

Seeing as the pinnacle of internet social success is the in-joke, it shouldn't come as a surprise that people will deliberately register domain names with double meanings and set up fake websites, so they can guffaw at the dullards who think they're real. These fake Slurls are related to the real thing, but are missing the most vital component: being unintentional. Like the

---

* "You don't know the difference? Oh my god you are such a newbie!" Kind of like that. Oh, alright: Rolling On Floor Laughing and Read The (ahem) Flipping Manual.

offspring of showbiz legends, they all too often fall far from the talent tree.

Fake Slurls tend to have one thing in common: thinly-veiled merchandise. You see, the second pillar of internet culture is commerce, in particular commerce that doesn't involve getting off your arse or doing anything useful. Merchandise offers an opportunity to make cash and spreads the sniggering into the real world—you can wear a t-shirt with a naughty slogan and no-one will notice, because they're not with the in-crowd, the idiots!

Let's get on with the fakes, but don't forget to check out the top gear on offer at the Slurls shop. We have some great apparel in men's *and* women's sizes, not to mention mugs, mouse mats, and engraved tankards. Not only will you look great, but you can show your stupid friends and family that you're in on the latest internet craze! Buy stuff now!

Pens Dipped In Chocolate

Pen Island is apparently the best place on the internet to get custom-made pens.

www.penisland.net

Pen Island is probably the best known Slurl that never was. So, what's wrong with it? Well, it's deliberate. Here's the evidence, culled from the site:

"Whether you're looking for a long and skinny pen, a thick pen, a fountain pen that squirts ink, or even a black pen, we have just the one for you."

Even a black pen? Golly, wouldn't that be exotic? And a pen that squirts ink is *very* useful. But wait, there's more:

"Just tell us a little bit about the size, colour, texture, and taste of the pen you're looking for, and we'll see what can do. You'll be surprised at what's available."

As far as I know texture and taste aren't normally selling points for pens. Still not convinced?

"Don't be ashamed if all you want is a normal skinny white pen, they get the job done and they are in fact our biggest seller! . . .

We've done it all. Wrapped in leather, little pink bows, we've even done pens dipped in chocolate!"

I rest my case.

Ferrets Make Great Pets

Ferreth and Jobs are—so they say—a law firm specialising in incorporation, litigation, patents, collections and contracts.

www.ferrethandjobs.com

At first I was taken in by this site. The typeface looks suitably formal and the declaration they have realised there is a problem is convincing, and hilarious:

"In other news, it has come to our attention that the domain name 'FerrethAndJobs.com' may be misread by some. We are currently investigating other options, but until then, we plan to continue our current branding in the hopes that clearer heads prevail. Any comments regarding the domain name itself may be directed to the individual who encouraged its use."

I like the idea of blaming their web designer, and encouraging legions of chortling visitors to go and taunt him instead of them. I also applaud the imagery, because ferrets really do make great pets—they're the third most popular in America after only cats and dogs. They are also used in "ferret therapy" in which their natural empathy and playfulness brings comfort to sick children and the depressed. If they could truly add hand jobs to their therapeutic range they would surely be number one. The problem is their mitts are a little small, and they have a habit of biting.

Sadly, the evidence of fakery stacks up quickly. Here is the low-down on my detective work:

❖ I was troubled by their tagline: "Is your business in the right hands?" For an outfit that may be mistaken for rodent masturbators, it's an awfully big coincidence.

❖ There is no information about the business on the site—not even where they are located. Googling "Ferreth and Jobs" returns nothing more; a real law firm would be in dozens of business directories.

❖ The only commerce being undertaken on the site is the sale of t-shirts for a fun run. Who would buy a shirt for a charity event that doesn't exist?*

❖ The "individual who encouraged its use" is actually registered as the *owner* of the site. This is our true architect, not the respectable attorneys at Ferreth and Jobs. They don't exist.

Nice try though.

---

* Smug propeller-heads who want to wear a top promoting ferret hand jobs without normal people noticing.

CHAPTER ELEVEN

Near Misses

Hunting down Slurls is not easy. In fact, it's near-impossible to find these rare critters. You can make up phrases and see if a matching site exists, but that almost never works. You can search for forums discussing Slurls and see if any new ones come up, but you normally find the same URLs over and over. Or you can sit back and wait for people to tell you about ones they stumbled across which, for me, has the best ratio of effort-to-Slurls.

Chance encounters also produce great stories about the moment when the realisation hit home—one poster was a web designer and worked on *northerngasheating.com* for days before the double meaning dawned on him. He fell into extended hysterics, while puzzled colleagues gawped. Another casually Googled their local bowling alley, and accidentally discovered *ilovebigals.com*.

Sadly, some submissions fall short of the mark. The worst rule-breakers are businesses who deliberately choose filthy puns for their names, and proudly slap them above their shop windows and in their website URLs. Like a relative who buys a pair of plastic tits and never takes them off, they grin like an imbecile every time you pass by.

Even if they don't break the rules outright, submitted Slurls can still inspire disdain by featuring poor spelling, sloppy grammar or fuzzy logic. We have seen some exceptional circumstances, where slight deficiencies can be overlooked, but most of the time these Slurls are ugly little toads that no minor royal can simply kiss into a prince.

Still, it's sometimes possible to overlook the slimy flesh and knobbly warts, and find a little joy among the also-rans. Here's a whistle-stop tour of the least-awful Slurls that never were.

Call a Spade a Spade, and a Ho a Hoe

Go Tahoe is the website of Lake Tahoe Incline Village and Crystal Bay Visitors Bureau, and it's jam-packed with information for visitors to this Californian lake.

www.gotahoe.com

This isn't a Slurl—because having a garden implement is not much of a social blunder—and the URL now redirects to:

www.gotahoenorth.com

Surely that is the last word, even for those who don't know their weeding tools from their sex workers. But hang on, there could be a knowing nod from the new website: it tells us that the local bus service is called Tahoe Area Regional Transportation—or TART for short.

Technology Is Evil

Teknor Apex Company is "an international compounder of advanced polymer materials." In other words, they make plastics and such.

www.teknorapex.com

Teknor Apex is a name so clumsy I can't help but suspect it was selected just to spell out "rape" when the two words are put together (of course it wasn't). For this to be a Slurl, "Tekno" and "X" would have to be words. They're not. And even if they were, the idea of "Tekno Rape X" doesn't work for me.

All's Fair in Love and War

The Battlefields Experience offers guided tours to areas of conflict in the Great War:

www.battlefieldsexperience.co.uk

It was suggested by Anonymous (he's a busy guy, I've seen his stuff everywhere). Imagining full-on rumpy in the midst of no-man's land does raise a smile, so why doesn't it count as a Slurl? Because "perience" isn't a word. Get a dictionary Anonymous.

A Seminal Performance

The Orchestra of the S.E.M. Ensemble, based in New York, was established in 1992 by Petr Kotik and performs new compositions for full orchestra.

www.semensemble.org

The *idea* of a semen semble Slurl is quite agreeable, because it sounds like some sort of artificial love-lubricant. But no matter how hard you try, it doesn't make a whole lot of sense.

Get Your Arse Into Gear

Utah company ARS Equipment's website provided information about its asphalt maintenance tools and services.

www.arsequipment.com

It's only one "e" away from a Slurl, but that's too far in my book. Which is a shame, as we surely need a site for arse equipment: either accessories for your bum, or equipment that's of really poor quality, as in the evocative phrase "a bunch of arse". Sadly, the site is no longer running—it disappeared in 2005.

And Up Yours Cynthia

This company farms freshwater pearls in China:

`www.fookyuepearl.com`

Yes, the Fook Yue Pearl Company has been engaged in manufacturing and wholesaling pearls for over 10 years. Its URL sounds like the utterance of an illiterate Mancunian who has a objection to someone called Pearl.

I can't help thinking of Liam Gallagher here—many people have been at the receiving end of his own very special brand of insults. To commemorate Oasis's umpteenth break-up, New Musical Express magazine (NME) published a list of "50 Incredulous Liam Gallagher Quotes". Here's a sample of his musings about fellow musical artistes:

- ❖ Ozzy Osbourne: ". . . a fooking mong . . ."
- ❖ Robbie Williams: ". . . somebody I'd like to hang."
- ❖ Keith Richards: ". . . jealous and senile . . ."
- ❖ Green Day's Billie Joe Armstrong: "I just don't like his head."

Whether you applaud Gallagher's frankness, or question the reliability of NME's reporting, compared to this bunch Pearl is getting off easy.

Accidentally on Purpose

Small businesses have long harnessed the power of the pun. Hairdressers are the worst offenders, regularly going with groansome names like *Hair Today*, *Short Cuts*, and *It's a Snip*. For some reason they seldom choose *Cubic Hair*, *Lunatic Fringe*, or *Cut and Run*. Here are the naughtiest domain names belonging to real-world businesses and clubs—they don't make the grade as Slurls because they are intentional:

www.thedirtyhoe.biz

A female landscape gardener from Seattle, Washington. If she goes missing from the job you'll probably find her on the nearest street corner.

www.beaverliquors.com *and* www.bungholeliquors.com

Two off-licenses, Beaver Liquors in Colorado and Bunghole Liquors in Massachusetts. Naïve visitors might think Bunghole Liquors is an innocent name (the bunghole is the hole in a barrel used to fill it) but the range of merchandise and tagline "We're Not Number 1 Butt We're Right Up There" should change their mind.

www.doggiestyles.co.uk

A mobile dog grooming service covering Warwickshire. The business is actually called Doggy Style, but that domain name was (unsurprisingly) unavailable. Aren't they embarrassed every time they answer the phone?

www.dirtydickscrabs.com

Incredibly, Dirty Dick's Crab House is a chain of four seafood restaurants in the southern United States. To hear about their soup of the day, they tell you to "Just ask Clappy". Why anyone would eat at a place with running jokes about sexually transmitted diseases is a mystery.

www.masterbaitonline.com

Master Bait and Tackle is a "cutting edge" fishing supplies shop in Florida. In this instance, cutting edge means "has a rude name" rather than its normal definition of, well, cutting edge.

www.upthebeavers.com

The website of a North London swimming club, nicknamed The Beavers. Unfortunately the Amateur Swimming Association (ASA) had a sense of humour bypass, and banned the site. How did The Beavers respond? They set up a fan site for the ASA official who banned them. In a strange way that makes me proud to be British.

Now You Show Me Yours

We've come to the end of our Slurls safari, and you can now consider yourself an expert. You know the rhyming rule for online exchanges and expresses. You've seen Americans gore foxes, crap metal and pee wine, like a Marilyn Manson concert sponsored by Jacob's Creek. When it comes to the Brits, they can play it subtle when the mood takes them. But they're apt to break wind at inappropriate times, and you don't even want to think about what happens when the drapes are closed.

The Cook Islands have shown how an entire country does Slurls with their legendary Dot Cock, and other nations have given generously too. Corporations have demonstrated that spending vast amounts of cash does not guarantee good—or even sane—results. The techies, bless 'em, know how to program in bits and bytes but can't see whores and rapists in their midst, even when equipped with arms full of whore presents and a rapist finder. Even kids haven't escaped, what with their swearing, stalking, shaving and, ah, slaughtering. And finally the fakes, which—irony of ironies—are even rarer than the sites they are trying to pass themselves off as. Where else is the copy rarer than the original?

So that's your lot. There must be more out there, but finding them is tough. Perhaps you can help? Do you sniff around the shady back alleys of the internet? Do you notice what's in your browser address bar? Would you know a Slurl if you found one?

Here's a quick recap:

a. There's a website *and*

b. It's an active website *and*

c. There's a double meaning *and*

d. It's not deliberate

    or

e. It's a fake

Got it? Yes? Good! Now put on your dirty-old-man's mac so you won't be recognised, grab a long stick to poke at grubby websites, fill your pockets with jelly babies for sustenance, and get hunting! Tell me about your finds by emailing *chief@slurls.com* or post a message in the *Suggest A Slurl* forum at *slurls.com*. You *will* be acknowledged for your efforts. Fame beckons!

Acknowledgements

This book would not have been possible without all the people who have discovered Slurls. Some were submitted to me directly via the website, and others were posted on the many blogs and forums where double-meaning domain names have been discussed. It would be impractical to honour you all here, and with names like BigGayDave and DwarfInABikini, look pretty silly, so I must thank all of you as a whole.

I'll make a single exception for Cheesemonkeh (I told you they had strange names), who posted about *pedo.org* on the delightfully named Facepunch discussion forum. The hapless Mr Monkeh was cross-examined on why he was looking up that particular URL (which is understandable) and may now have received a few real Facepunches in his furry little bonce.

The web boasts some superb free reference sites, and I found The Internet Archive and DomainTools particularly valuable. Using these I could identify domain name owners; discover when URLs were first registered; and see how sites looked several years ago—even ones that no longer exist.

Wikipedia also helped enormously, with essays on main-stream topics such as the detailed plot of Japanese tentacle-rape porno cartoons—saving me from the disturbing (and possibly illegal) experience of watching them myself. No wonder the *Encyclopaedia Britannica* is in decline, when kids can get their hands on that kind of quality knowledge for free.

A big thank you to everyone who spared their precious time to read and feedback on various drafts of the book. So that's Tim, Kim, Sam and Guy. I also had help from people with names more than three letters long (show-offs): Jaime, Tracy and Andy.

Most of all, I owe a debt of gratitude to my wonderful wife Tracy for her time proofreading and advising. Without her help *Slurls* could never have reached the standards of finesse and decency it has been able to sink to. Let's celebrate with a big night out! I've heard good things about the food at *Dirty Dick's Crabs*. We could have a drink of *IP Wine,* or some *Beaver Liquor*, then go dancing at *Holland's Hit Festival*. Whatever we choose, it will definitely be a night to remember.

Index of Websites

The Website of the Book of the Website

The Slurls website at *www.slurls.com* is the spiritual home of the dirty double-meaning domain name. Scholarly insights into these web addresses can only be found in this book, but the Slurls website is the best place to give feedback, discuss, criticise and generally get involved. Feel free to drop in and experience a hearty welcome to the community.

About the Author

Andy Geldman first came across unintentionally hilarious website addresses in 2006 and quickly coined the word "Slurl"—a combination of "slur" and URL—to describe the phenomenon. The Slurls website came soon after and served to show off the latest URLs found through Andy's own efforts or submitted by visitors. When not hunting for Slurls he works as a freelance software developer and writes his blog *Who Ate All The Cookies?*

Lightning Source UK Ltd.
Milton Keynes UK
30 April 2010

153557UK00001B/73/P